5/98

An American
Daughter

WENDY

WASSERSTEIN

An American Daughter

HARCOURT BRACE & COMPANY

New York   San Diego   London

Requests for permission to make copies of any part of the work should be mailed to: Permissions Department, Harcourt Brace & Company, 6277 Sea Harbor Drive, Orlando, Florida 32887-6777.

Photographs copyright © 1996 by Joan Marcus

"You're sixteen (You're Beautiful and you're mine)" (Bob Sherman, Dick Sherman) © 1960 (renewed) Warner-Tamerlane Publishing Corp. (BMI) & MWAC Music (BMI) All rights administered by Warner-Tamerlane Publishing Corp. All Rights Reserved. Used by Permission. "Love Me Tender" by Elvis Presley and Vera Matson Copyright © 1956 by Elvis Presley Music, Inc. All administrative rights for the world controlled by R&H Music. Copyright Renewed. International Copyright Secured. Reprinted by Permission. All Rights Reserved. Excerpt from "The Fourth of July" in *The Mind Reader* copyright © 1974 by Richard Wilbur, reprinted by permission of Harcourt Brace & Company.

Library of Congress Cataloging-in-Publication Data
Wasserstein, Wendy.
An American daughter/Wendy Wasserstein.—1st ed.
p.   cm.
ISBN 0-15-100332-7
1. United States—Officials and employees—Selection and appointment—Drama.   2. Fathers and daughters—United States—Drama.
3. Women in politics—United States—Drama.   I.Title.
PS3573.A798A8   1998
812'.54—dc21   97-36079

Text set in Sabon
Designed by Ivan Holmes
Printed in the United States of America
First edition
F E D C B A

For Michael Kinsley

Looking back at the relatively brief New York run of *An American Daughter*, my old friend and producer, André Bishop, the artistic director of Lincoln Center Theater, said to me, "The incredible thing about this play is that your life and that of the main character merged. It's as if you had a premonition."

Actually, it isn't incredible to me. My plays seem to have an instinct for proving true. After I finished *The Heidi Chronicles*, many single women I knew began adopting children, which is Heidi's choice in the final scene. On the opening night of *The Sisters Rosensweig* on Broadway, I met the English theater director Nicholas Hytner, who had studied at Cambridge and had directed a musical version of *The Scarlet Pimpernel*—exactly as Geoffrey Duncan, the successful English theater director, in my play, did. The things I dream about often do come true, though usually not for me.

I generally get an idea for a new play just as I am completing one. It works almost like a dialectic or, to be less pretentious, like a response to what I'm doing. Anyone who writes a carefully-structured comedy like *The Sisters Rosensweig* is bound to come up against the criticism, both external and gnawingly internal, of "When are you going to stretch and show us your anger? When will you grow and reveal your serious side?" Anne Cattaneo, the dramaturg of Lincoln Center Theater, always pipes in with "When will you show us your dark side?"

But a writer doesn't grow just to prove she is capable of higher jumps or new tricks. On the contrary, I believe the content must dictate the form. During the year *The Sisters Rosensweig* was on Broadway, I came up against obstacles, particularly female ones, that I had known about intellectually but never felt myself. My sister Sandra was diagnosed with breast cancer, and at the same time I was attempting, in vain, to have a child. I spent months, years, in waiting rooms, surrounded now by women in wigs on their way to chemotherapy, now by women with cell phones and attachés waiting to hear if their blood count was still in the ballpark for bearing children. The simultaneous situations certainly redefined for me "having it all."

The inevitable result of this experience was that I wanted to organize the sadness, frustration, and truth of it into play form. I have always written to find out what I'm thinking and, if not to look for answers, then at least to attempt to ask the question.

It's a great mistake to view comedic writing as a comforter cloaking an excruciating bed of nails. And, in my opinion, it is an even greater mistake to dismiss witty repartee as just a series of one-liners. My intention with *An American Daughter* was not to overhaul but to widen the range of my work: to create a fractured fairy tale depicting both a social and a political dilemma for contemporary professional women. In other words, if Chekhov was the icon of *The Sisters Rosensweig*, then Ibsen would be the postfeminist muse of *An American*

Daughter. The topicality of the play would be merely a container for a deeper problem.

The initial inspiration for the story, of a surgeon general nominee whose confirmation unravels because of a serious oversight, came from events in the first hundred days of the Clinton Administration. During that time, Zoe Baird, a talented Washington lawyer turned corporate counsel, was nominated for attorney general. Ms. Baird seemed to embody "having it all." She was a successful attorney, the wife of a Yale Law School professor, and the mother of a young son. But during her Senate confirmation hearing, the information came out that she had hired illegal aliens for child care.

Suddenly "Nannygate" erupted. From being a role model, Ms. Baird became the embodiment of privilege, affluence, and the foibles of a generation. After weeks of scrutiny, she removed her name from nomination, as did the following two, female, nominees. Judge Kimba Wood also came under fire for her child-care arrangements and Professor Lani Guinier was told that her radical views on race and election reform would make her confirmation impossible.

A few months before Nannygate, Hillary Rodham Clinton, then the wife of a presidential nominee, appeared on national television and made the fatal error of admitting that she didn't want to stay at home and bake cookies. There was uproar, and the next time we saw Mrs. Clinton, she was wearing a headband and holding her husband's hand. In other words, we hadn't come such a long way, baby. In my mind there was a connection between the image of the chastened first-lady-to-be and the attorney general who tried so hard to do it all that she missed a glaring detail. They were both accomplished professional women who seemed completely prepared for life's obstacles. Whereas their contemporary femininity seemed at first their strength, it became their downfall.

An American Daughter is set in Washington and therefore includes both politicians and the press. The nominee, Dr. Lyssa Dent Hughes, is the daughter of a Republican senator from Indiana and a descendant of Ulysses S. Grant. One of Lyssa's best friends, and a best friend of her husband, Walter, is Morrow McCarthy, an ultraconservative gay pundit. Walter's prize student is Quincy Quince, a neofeminist who looks askance at Lyssa's generation as "earnest do-gooders." Lyssa becomes the subject of a television news magazine, *Time Zone*, and her interviewer, Timber Tucker, tries to make the coveted interview further his career.

It's difficult for an author to say exactly what her play is about. That's better left to audiences and drama critics. Some critics decided that my play was about far too much. Was it about politics? Was it an attack on the media? Was it about women? Frankly, I believe that the major events of a person's life are seldom about "one thing." Did Lyssa Hughes throw a jury-duty notice away because she was an overcommitted professional woman or because of her arrogant belief that her "good works" meant she did not have to bother with small bureaucratic details? Did her husband reveal her minor misdemeanor because he felt threatened by her or because intellectual points were more important to him than emotional ones? At the end of the play, Walter tells Lyssa, "We're smart people. . . . We deserve to have gotten everything out of [life] that the really smart ones get." Perhaps this play is about the aspirations, sadness, defeats, and accomplishments of "really smart people." That is, perhaps it is about character.

Over the years I've begun to feel a political claustrophobia in the American theater. Even in the most challenging plays, those on the right are in the wrong and those on the left are crusading for good. I wanted to mix things up a bit. The old senator is an opponent of a woman's right to an abortion but also is the father of a leading pro-choice advocate. The gay journalist is his best friend's confidant but also the one who destroys her career. The young feminist is the hope of a movement but also a narcissistic woman driven by ambition. If my writing was going to stretch, I wanted the theater's political correctness to stretch with it.

The play was first read at Lincoln Center with Meryl Streep as Lyssa, and done at The Seattle Rep in a workshop production, again with Meryl. That Seattle workshop, with my constant collaborator, Daniel Sullivan, directing, was one of my most satisfying theatrical experiences. The play evolved in a significant way, and both Cotter Smith and Penny Fuller—as Timber and Chubby, respectively—came with it to New York.

Opening a play directly on Broadway, even under the auspices of a nonprofit organization like Linclon Center, is a terrifying prospect. In this case we had a wonderful cast, including Kate Nelligan, Hal Holbrook, Lynne Thigpen, Peter Riegert, Bruce Norris, and Elizabeth Marvel. But the pressure of a Broadway preview is overwhelming, and the opinions are endless. We cut, we pasted, we condensed, and by opening night I was quite proud of our production. Kate Nelligan had me come to her dressing room to tell me, "Did you know this play would change your life? Now you will be taken seriously as a playwright." Well, I thought I had been taken seriously, but I knew what she meant. This play, more than my others, is a play of ideas. Pat Collins, the noblest of lighting designers, would sidle up to me during tech rehearsals and whisper, "No one else is saying this!"

I have never had such a varied reception of a play. Reviews, good and bad, are part of the process of playwriting. What was odd about this play was that the gender issue became so important. I received letters from countless women (some quite famous, some not) telling me how much this play meant to them, and Linda Winer, the drama critic at *Newsday,* and one of the few female critics, wrote that it was my best play.

For many women *An American Daughter* wasn't about too many things; it was, rather, about *the* thing. But to some men, and many critics, it seemed the rantings of a comedic writer trying to find something "important" to say. As weeks passed after the opening, I felt more and more like Dr. Lyssa Dent Hughes on *Time Zone,* flanked by her father and husband, who both meant well, respected her, but just didn't get it. It's a terrifyingly lonely position. I was racked by self-doubt yet amazed by my own strength to cope with the negativity. I still don't know if the problem was that the issues in the play were too close to the bone or that I simply couldn't handle them.

One morning during the run of the play, still in bed, I read in a theatrical gossip column that I had "slipped on a banana peel this season" but would receive a Tony nomination anyway because "everyone loves Wendy." Perhaps that was the day when Lyssa and I completed our merger. There's something about being a woman that makes it all personal.

I was not nominated for a Tony Award, proof that everyone, thank heaven, does not love Wendy. But Lynne Thigpen for her performance as Dr. Judith B. Kaufman was and she won! Of all my characters, the African-American Jewish oncologist is the one emotionally closest to me. Perhaps I was hiding behind this woman in order not to reveal my own anger, but that sounds like a nice topic for a joint psychology-and-theater senior paper.

A final word about this play and two men. Dr. Judith is named for my cousin the late Barry Kaufman, who taught African-American studies in the New York City public school system. The play is dedicated to Michael Kinsley, the journalist who taught me about the Washington press, integrity, and the true purpose of intelligence: to observe keenly and love committedly.

I do have a theory about writing for the theater. If you aim for a six and get a six, you'll do fine. If you aim for a ten and get a six, or even an eight, you won't do well at all. But I believe the purpose of writing plays, or practising any art form, is to try for a ten every time.

At the curtain of act one, Lyssa asks Judith, "What gives you the audacity to believe you've failed if you can't make life or stop death?" Judith, who has just been to the Festival of Regrets by the banks of the Potomac, replies simply, "Because I was taught if I was a good girl and I worked hard, I could." After she withdraws her nomination, Lyssa is given a letter by her father from Ulysses S. Grant to his daughter urging her to "rise and continue." I look forward to *An American Daughter* rising and continuing.

An American
Daughter

ACT ONE

A Saturday in September. Around noon. A living room leading to a garden of a Georgetown house. LYSSA DENT HUGHES, *a forty-two-year-old woman in a cotton shirt and jeans, is watching herself on the television news.*

LYSSA *on television:* Good health care begins with education. For example, both women and men need to learn to recognize the symptoms of heart disease. Advancing health care is a matter of advancing scientific knowledge but, just as important, advancing every individual's knowledge. As physician to the nation, I will be in a unique position to further this administration's goal that every American, male or female, adult or child, has access to the best heal . . . excuse me . . . the best health care information. The Surgeon General has the opportunity to educate every American about their individual health. The greatest protection is prevention.

ANCHORMAN'S VOICE: Elsewhere in the news, a fire broke out this morning at a Bethesda florist . . .

LYSSA *turns off the television and starts picking up toys.*

LYSSA: ... the best health care information ...

BOY'S VOICE *from upstairs:* Mom, Mom ... you made a mistake.

LYSSA: Tell me I was great.

BOY'S VOICE: Information ...

LYSSA: Yeah, I know, but just tell me I was great.

BOY'S VOICE: You were great.

LYSSA: Thank you. I was great.

LYSSA *turns on the radio.* "It's Washington DC, home of the oldies, and you're sixteen, you're beautiful, and you're you-know-who's on WOLD 91.3." *Song begins,* "You walked out of my dreams into my arms, now you're my angel divine." *She begins to dance along.* QUINCY QUINCE, *a very pretty woman of about twenty-seven in a miniskirt and leather bomber jacket, enters the living room from the garden.*

QUINCY: Classic rock. Very simple. Very pure. Very paternal.

LYSSA *turns off the radio:* Imagine wanting "to come on like a dream, peaches and cream, lips like strawberry wine." *She stretches out her hand:* I'm Quincy Quince. You left the garden gate open. I'm here for Walter.

LYSSA: I'm afraid Walter's not home. He's at the Air and Space Museum with one of our boys. Can I help you?

QUINCY: I love the Air and Space Museum. I'm an aviatrix nut. Women in the twenties and thirties were able to excel in show business, cosmetology, and aviation. There's a chapter in my new book about flight and sexuality.

LYSSA: Walter should be back in a little while. I'll tell him you dropped by.

QUINCY: I love that Dr. Lyssa Hughes does her own cleaning on the day of her nomination. I love that! *She takes a bag of raisins from her purse.* Raisin? I also have baby carrots. I always carry snacks and water.

LYSSA: How do you know my husband?

QUINCY: I'm sorry. I thought you recognized me. I'm Quincy Quince. I wrote *The Prisoner of Gender*.

LYSSA: Oh, of course! You're Walter's celebrity student. The rebirth of feminism.

QUINCY: "Sexism made simple."

LYSSA: We saw you on *Late Night with Conan O'Brien*. Most of Walter's students don't make it to late night.

QUINCY: Walter is brilliant! He's the only academic who can reshape liberalism into an active stance instead of a do-gooder whine. Walter is the only man who "gets it."

LYSSA: You're much kinder to him than I am.

QUINCY: And you're much different than I expected.

LYSSA: I am?

QUINCY: You have more bite. I thought you'd be sweeter. Sweet women are really very angry people. They're trapped by their own repressed hostility.

LYSSA: Usually I am sweeter. I just didn't know you'd be coming. I hope Walter hasn't forgotten his appointment with you.

QUINCY: Actually Walter didn't know I'd be coming. I'm in Washington doing the usual round of book signing and talk shows. But we had a few cancellations due to the Jewish holidays. I can't wait to get back on the air and talk about meeting you.

LYSSA: Please say that I'm not so nice. Say I have bite.

QUINCY: I'll say that the future Surgeon General is one of the truly empowered, self-actualized real women.

JUDITH B. KAUFMAN, *forty-two, an African-American woman in a floral skirt and tweed jacket, enters. She is boisterous and energetic.*

JUDITH: How many times have I told you if you insist on leaving your gate open, it's an open invitation for any schvartze on the street. They could just waltz right into your garden and walk off with your children, your furniture, and your raisins. *She picks up the raisins and kisses* LYSSA. Happy New Year, honey.

LYSSA: Isn't it a little early?

JUDITH: Okay. Happy High Holidays. There were two African Americans at the Washington Hebrew Congregation today—the rabbi's chauffeur and me. And when that rabbi blew his chauffeur in front of the entire congregation, I said to myself, Judith, next year in Jerusalem.

LYSSA: Quincy, this is my oldest friend, Dr. Judith B. Kaufman. Quincy wrote *The Prisoner of Gender.*

JUDITH: Of course, Quincy Quince. The next generation of feminists.

QUINCY: Are you ob-gyn?

JUDITH: No, I'm the other kind of woman's doctor. Oncology. Breast cancer. But it's possible I could have specialized in something women don't have, like heads, necks, or throats.

QUINCY: But you're doing the important work.

The phone rings.

LYSSA *picks up the phone:* Hello, Dad! You're back! Yeah. Just a sec, let me go to another phone. *She puts him on hold and says to* JUDITH: The Senator's back from his honeymoon.

JUDITH: Did they get it annulled?

LYSSA: Quincy, just think of my friend Judith's hostility as her overtly repressed sweetness. *She exits.*

QUINCY: How does Lyssa's father feel about her nomination?

JUDITH: Senator Hughes has almost a quarter century's unblemished record of robbing from the poor to give to the rich. How do you think he feels about his daughter the bleeding heart? It's a low blow to the memory of Lyssa's great-great-granddaddy.

QUINCY: You mean Ulysses S. Grant? Walter used to talk about that in class all the time.

JUDITH: Your Walter married well.

QUINCY: He's not my Walter. He's my mentor.

JUDITH: Shame on you, Quincy. You didn't have a female mentor.

QUINCY: I think we're at a place now where we can look beyond gender for mentors.

JUDITH: I think we can look beyond or around gender for anything except prostate and ovarian cancer. Does your "Quincy" mean there's a president lurking in your bloodline also?

QUINCY: Our real name was Quintopolous. We're Greek. My father changed it to Quince when he noticed the jelly at a breakfast function. He's a party consultant in Astoria, Queens.

JUDITH: You mean he owns a coffee shop and caters office platters.

QUINCY: And your father? My book after the next one will be about fathers and daughters.

JUDITH: My father was a French teacher at Boys' High, Brooklyn. Boys were pulling knives on each other in homeroom and my dad taught them to say "pardonnez-moi." They shipped me off to Miss Porter's boarding school. That's where I met Lyssa.

QUINCY: Your mother didn't mind.

JUDITH: My mother believed only art and education made life tolerable. She was a Baptist piano teacher from Tuscaloosa, Alabama. Her family never forgave her for moving north with a Freedom Rider Jew.

QUINCY: So you're not technically Jewish because you're mother isn't.

JUDITH: I am, technically. I was bat mitzvahed at Garfield Temple, Garfield Place, Brooklyn, New York. Today I am a woman. I thank God every day I was born half a man.

QUINCY: I learned from my mother that a woman's life can have no boundaries.

JUDITH: Do you mind if I lie down?

QUINCY: Should I get Lyssa? Are you not feeling well?

JUDITH: Quincy, time will teach you that a woman's life is all about boundaries. Would you mind passing me that pillow? Organized religion always gives me a migraine.

QUINCY: I see life completely differently than you do.

JUDITH: Diversity is the succor of the nineties.

LYSSA *re-enters.*

LYSSA: Daddy's bringing Charlotte to my televised brunch tomorrow. Have you ever heard of a television reporter called Lumber Tucker?

QUINCY: You mean Timber Tucker. He's on that newsmagazine *Time Zone.* He did a great piece on the women of Sarajevo. He's a hero of the Gulf War.

LYSSA: Well, apparently the President's press secretary has convinced Timber and *Time Zone* to do a puff piece on me.

JUDITH: This is going to make really boring television.

LYSSA: Judith, if I have to explain to Timber Tucker over pancakes that gun control is really a health issue, it's worth it to me. And if he wants to watch me pick up my kids from soccer practice so every woman in this country is assured reproductive freedom, it's also worth it to me. And I happen to know it's worth it to you too.

QUINCY: I was so proud when you mentioned reproductive rights at the White House this morning.

JUDITH: Were you at that breakfast?

QUINCY: No. But women's issues are my priority.

JUDITH: Did you hear that, Lyssa? The rest of us can all relax now.

LYSSA: Judith, please!

JUDITH: I'm sorry.

LYSSA: Quincy was one of Walter's best students. And I know my husband thinks your work is very impressive.

JUDITH: I'm sorry. Lyssa knows I get a little nuts when things are too important to me.

QUINCY: It's important to all of us. I hope Timber Tucker knows that. I mean I'd love to talk to him about Dr. Hughes from a younger woman's perspective.

JUDITH: Maybe you should come back here for brunch tomorrow. You haven't had brunch in Georgetown till you've tried Lyssa's homemade scones. Lyssa?

LYSSA: Absolutely. Come to brunch. Walter will be happy to see you.

QUINCY: I can't believe you make your own scones!

LYSSA: Yes, and I built that fireplace from scratch.

QUINCY: Are you sure you want to share this important time with me?

LYSSA: Sure.

QUINCY *opens her appointment book:* What time are they all coming tomorrow? Because I may have to do a little juggling.

LYSSA: We generally do brunch at about one.

QUINCY: I'll work it out. It's been a real honor to meet you. I
just want to thank you for all the amazing work you've
been doing.

LYSSA: You're welcome.

QUINCY: No, really. You put women's health-care issues on the
map. I'll be having a wonderful life because of you. *She
shakes* JUDITH's *hand.* It's been a pleasure meeting you too.
I hope you feel better. *She exits.*

JUDITH: Why won't she have a wonderful life because of *me?*
She hits LYSSA *with a pillow.* Why isn't she happy to have
the opportunity to thank *me? She hits her again.* Why does
it always have to be *you?*

LYSSA: Why did *you* have to invite her back here for brunch?
She hits JUDITH.

JUDITH: It's New Year's. I felt guilty. I was awful to her. Why
didn't you stop me?

LYSSA: Who could stop you?

JUDITH: I behaved like a cow. An old and bitter, envious cow.

LYSSA: Let it go. You'll buy her a pony tomorrow.

JUDITH: Lyssa, do you know what holy Taschlich is?

LYSSA: Something floating in a soup?

JUDITH: Taschlich is the Festival of Regrets. It happens a day
after New Year's, when good Jews send 365 days' worth
of their sins and sadness out to sea. The upper echelons
toss baguette crumbs and rosemary croutons of sorrow into
the Potomac, while those of us still toiling for the public
good fling yesterday's fat-free muffins. I will now be adding
to my list of sins Miss Quincy Quince. Do you have any
regrets, Lyssa, that you'd like me to set sail for you tomorrow?

LYSSA: *Remembrance of Things Past.* I should have finished it.

JUDITH: I regret my life, Lyssa. I can't believe I let the time go by.

LYSSA: You didn't let the time go by. You're a remarkable doctor.

JUDITH: A patient with bones like Swiss cheese asked me the other day when we would next be changing courses. I said, for perhaps the thousandth time in my career, "Well, Mrs. Mandell, it's like playing a fish. We'll watch where it swims and take it from there." What I didn't tell Mrs. Mandell is that the one certainty we have is this particular fish will painfully and untimely stop swimming.

LYSSA: I wish you would allow someone to cherish you.

JUDITH: I'm in no state of mind to be cherished. Especially by me.

LYSSA: But maybe this will be a good year.

JUDITH: Yes, and maybe there'll be a pill that makes white chocolate mousse the same calories as raw fennel. Maybe even sperm catalogue specimen 1147 will scramble up a few eggs with a nice Jewish African-American doctor.

LYSSA: You know that at some point very soon you really have to put an end to this.

JUDITH: Why? Abraham had a child at one hundred.

LYSSA: I'm serious. For five years you've endured every in vitro and hormone treatment known to modern medicine. You're a very good doctor. What do you think this has all done to your system? Never mind your mental health.

JUDITH: I really don't want to talk about this right now.

LYSSA: You brought it up.

JUDITH: In jest. Then in true Lyssa fashion you turned it into a public issue.

LYSSA: This is not a public issue! You're my oldest friend. You're much too valuable to continue doing this to yourself. All lives don't have to be about children.

JUDITH: How would you know?

"I'm in no state of mind to be cherished. Especially by me."
(Lynn Thigpen, Kate Nelligan)

Pause.

LYSSA: Oh, Judy. I'm so sorry.

JUDITH: You're the only person I know who dares to call me Judy.

LYSSA: That's because when I met you your name was Judy.

JUDITH: I'll know in a week. And then I promise I'll be sending that particular five-year cycle of great expectations and regret out to sea. Don't you just love being around me these days. I know I do.

LYSSA: Yes, you're a lot of fun.

JUDITH: Maybe you're right. Maybe this could be a very good year.

LYSSA: Maybe, just maybe, this time one tiny spermatozoid will take a look at your highly desirable eggs and say, "Hi there, cutie!"

JUDITH: You're not sixteen. You're not beautiful. But you're mine.

LYSSA: I was just singing that. Isn't that odd! After all these years we're still on the same wavelength.

JUDITH: It was on the "I refuse to believe I'm middle-aged and the culture isn't about me anymore" radio station when I was pulling up. I hate to disappoint you.

LYSSA: You never disappoint me. *Begins to sing slowly:* "You stepped out of my dreams and into my car, now you're my angel divine."

JUDITH *harmonizes as they both sing.*

JUDITH & LYSSA: "You're sixteen, you're beautiful and you're mine."

Saturday night. Around 7:30. WALTER ABRAHMSON, *forty-seven, is smoking and watching television.*

ANCHORMAN: The President reconfirmed his commitment to education yesterday by visiting the Chevy Chase School. The President attended assembly and a school lunch. Also, confirming yesterday's rumors, Dr. Lyssa Dent Hughes ...

WALTER: Lyssa!

ANCHORMAN: ... accepted the nomination to be Surgeon General following a White House breakfast this morning.

WALTER: Lyssa! Lyssa! You bumped Rwanda.

ANCHORMAN: Dr. Hughes is the daughter of Republican Senator Alan Hughes of Indiana ...

BOY'S VOICES FROM UPSTAIRS: But Mom ...

LYSSA *coming down the stairs:* I'll play Space Invaders with you later. *She enters the living room.*

ANCHORMAN: ... and a former college classmate of the First Lady. Following the death of Surgeon General Dr. David Burns, in a plane crash, and the defeated nomination of Dr. Charles McDermott, Dr. Hughes is expected to have a swift confirmation. According to Capitol Hill insiders she's

a popular choice with both pro-choice soccer moms and
more conservative fast-food dads.

WALTER *suddenly yells at the television.*

WALTER: The point is, doofus, she's a popular choice because
  she has a record as a brilliant health-care administrator.
  The point is she still believes public health is good
  government.
LYSSA: I'm warning you, you shouldn't smoke.
WALTER: You're not the Surgeon General yet. I don't understand you. Why doesn't this make you crazy?
LYSSA: He didn't really say anything.
WALTER: Lyssa, don't fall into a trap. The problem is they
  want you for all the wrong reasons. You're just like that
  breath mint.
LYSSA: What breath mint?
WALTER: The one that's also a candy mint. The Senator makes
  you okay with the right-wing Nazis and your politics make
  you a pinup for the do-gooder Commies.
LYSSA: And if I could only soothe sore throats, I could be three
  mints in one. Why not make the third-party cuckoos happy
  too?
WALTER: I'm making a valid point here. Lizard, no compro-
  mise candidate can get the important work done.
LYSSA: You sound like a right-to-lifer.
WALTER: Honey, don't be naive.
LYSSA: Walter, you're the dean of naive. You're the author of
  Towards a Lesser Elite.
WALTER: The question is, Lizard, "What do you really want
  to do?"
LYSSA: Walter, you know exactly what I want to do.

WALTER: What? Make the world a better place? Do good on a grand scale? Teach the world to sing in perfect harmony? They'll never let you get away with it. Look what happened to national health insurance.

LYSSA: All right. I want to make heaps of money, get our children into Harvard, and have upper arms that don't jiggle. What do you want to do, sweetie?

WALTER: I want to be invited to Winona Ryder's next dinner party and be mistaken for someone her age. I want to conduct *Il Travatore* to a standing ovation and come home and have sex on the dashboard of a '68 Chevy. I want to be the focus of attention. I want to make you happy.

LYSSA: I am happy, Walter. I'm always happy.

WALTER: I thought you were brilliant at that breakfast this morning. If we weren't married, I would have hustled you right into the Lincoln bedroom.

LYSSA: Walter, we don't have that kind of money.... God damn it! Why don't your sons ever bother to put their shoes away?

WALTER: Why don't you sit down, honey? I'll put the kids' damn shoes away.

LYSSA: Do you know where they go?

WALTER: Sure. In the dishwasher. Did Kip say he had a good time with me today?

LYSSA: Uh-huh. Great.

WALTER: It's amazing how much Kip is like me. He's very sensitive. Very imaginative. You should have heard the stories he made up about the Space Shuttle. He's hilarious. Nicholas is much more like you. He's perfectly happy home alone with his computer.

LYSSA: Are you saying he's pedantic, just like his mother?

WALTER: Don't be so defensive, honey.

LYSSA: You just told me that one of our children is funny and imaginative like you and the other is humorless and academic like me.

WALTER: I think this job thing is making you a little nutso. Look, worst-case scenario: if it doesn't happen, I won't be profiled as one of the most enlightened husbands in America. So what? Even in your present overworked and highly emotional condition, I'll still love you.

LYSSA: Shut up, Walter.

WALTER: I'm just trying to be supportive. I'm so proud of you.

LYSSA: Walter, have you ever regretted your life?

WALTER: Looking back, I would have tried to have sex with Joanie Tenzer in high school instead of being terrified of her.

LYSSA: At forty-seven, Joanie Tenzer is your one regret?

WALTER *singing:* "Love me, Tenzer, love me do." What's there to regret? I love you, I love our kids, I love my books, I love how we live.

LYSSA: Judith regrets her life.

WALTER: Judith is on mega-doses of insane fertility drugs. She's not just angry. She's an accident waiting to happen.

LYSSA: Your friend Quincy Quince says anger is healthy. She says sweetness is a camouflage for repressed hostility.

WALTER: Have you been reading *The Prisoner of Gender?*

LYSSA: No. She made a guest appearance in your garden today.

WALTER: Quincy was here? In our garden?

LYSSA: Yup.

WALTER: And you forgot to tell me? I deeply regret that.

LYSSA: Judith hated her.

WALTER: Judith has no right to pass judgment on someone as valuable as Quincy. Quincy's committed to making a tired ideology new. Did she say when she'll be back?

"What's there to regret? I love you, I love our kids, I love my books, I love how we live." (Peter Reigert, Kate Nelligan)

LYSSA: Tomorrow for brunch, to meet Daddy and some reporter who's doing a piece on the family.

WALTER: He's doing a piece on this family? Why wasn't I told?

LYSSA: Oh, he just wants to meet the famous in the family.

WALTER: *Towards a Lesser Elite* is still a standard text in more than three thousand colleges. Even that I was recently featured in a "Where Are They Now?" column. *He picks up the telephone.* Maybe this reporter doesn't even know we're married.

LYSSA: Of course he knows we're married. Who are you calling?

WALTER: Morrow. Maybe he'd like to come.

LYSSA: Walter ...

WALTER *on the phone:* Morrow, Lyssa and I want to invite you over to meet a hunky television reporter. Call us. *He hangs up.*

LYSSA: Jesus ...

WALTER: What's the matter?

LYSSA: Do you really want Morrow to be here with that reporter?

WALTER: Why not? Because he's gay?

LYSSA: Walter, don't be ridiculous. I love Morrow, but his new antiabortion stand is not exactly how I want to represent myself.

WALTER: It's not new. He's always had his faith.

LYSSA: I just wish he'd find a boyfriend and leave women's reproductive rights alone. Do you realize we've known him more than ten years and he's never shown up here with a man.

WALTER: So he keeps his personal life separate from us.

LYSSA: Walter, as Morrow would say, "Hello," we *are* his personal life.

WALTER: I'll call him back and cancel.

LYSSA: Don't. He'll only get paranoid. I'm going upstairs. I promised the kids I would play Space Invaders with them.

WALTER: I don't hear them complaining.

LYSSA: That's because by now they're probably on the Internet with a transvestite in Bucharest.

WALTER *hugs her:* What's this?

LYSSA: What do you mean "What's this"? A Gap cotton blend, $39.95.

WALTER: And what's under this?

LYSSA: Olga 34B, fifteen bucks on sale at Nordstrom's.

WALTER: Can I see?

LYSSA: Walter ...

WALTER: I saw you give birth to twins. I think you can show me your Olga 34B, fifteen bucks on sale at Nordstrom's.

LYSSA: Honey, let's go upstairs.

WALTER: I don't want to go upstairs. There are Space Invaders and nannies and grown-up things up there. How 'bout the car?

LYSSA: The Volvo?

WALTER: I've got the latest Big Head Todd.

LYSSA: What's a Big Head Todd?

WALTER: Lyssa, there's actual music past Aretha Franklin and the Beatles.

LYSSA: But I don't like music past Aretha Franklin and the Beatles.

WALTER: You're not even curious anymore. You want to know why I'm so taken with Quincy and Morrow? They're looking directly at the future. You're as rooted as any ardent right-winger.

LYSSA: Are you constantly renewing yourself?

WALTER: I don't know what the hell I'm doing. But I'll be damned before I get old and boring and fat.

LYSSA: How could you get fat, Walter? You run daily from here to Virginia.

WALTER *pulls up his shirt:* Feel that.

LYSSA: Flat.

WALTER *makes a muscle:* Feel this.

LYSSA: Mmmm. Also flat. Walter, you have the strong virile arms of a twenty-eight-year-old male hustler. No, a Green Beret. Walter, you should have been a Green Beret instead of a conscientious objector. I'm sorry, honey. I'm sorry. *She unbuttons her shirt.* Hi, I don't know if you remember me. My name is Joanie Tenzer. Lyssa had to leave suddenly on sabbatical. Whatever that means.

WALTER: Hi, Joanie. Nice to see you. It's been a long time.

LYSSA: I hear you've got a Big Head Todd. Can we go to your car and listen to it?

WALTER: Joanie, what do you want to listen to that junk for? Have I ever told you that according to my college roommate, Dr. Martin Brody, Professor of Harmony at Wellesley College, the Beach Boys are the most sophisticated American composers since Gershwin?

LYSSA: Gosh, Walter, you know everything. I didn't even know you had a college roommate. But maybe that's because I've been in high school for the past thirty years.

WALTER: Take for example "California Girls."

LYSSA: Okay.

WALTER: Listen to this. *He puts on "California Girls." He looks at her.* Joanie.

LYSSA: Yes, Walter.

WALTER: That Olga looks like it comes from a nunnery.

LYSSA: It's from Nordstrom's. It lifts and separates.

WALTER: Joanie.

LYSSA: Yes, Walter.

WALTER: Could you send Lyssa back in here. *He kisses her.* I love you Lyssa Dent Hughes. Of all the choices I've made, the one I'll never regret is marrying you.

Sunday morning. JUDITH *enters through the front door.* MOR-
ROW MCCARTHY *enters from the kitchen, carrying five Sunday
papers.* MORROW *is thirty and looks younger, in a casual but
studied fashion. He wears retro-fifties clothes. As they enter the
room, we hear a Sunday Public Radio voice-over.*

PUBLIC RADIO VOICE: Perhaps the greatest debate in the country this week will not be welfare reform but whether the
President should adopt a dog or a cat as his best friend
in the White House. A nationwide telepoll is accepting
1-800-VOTE C.A.T. or D.O.G. calls till 9 P.M. Friday.

MORROW *puts down the paper he's been reading:* He's such
a policy wonk. A Harvard-educated policy wonk. He may
be the commander-in-chief, but he still needs a poll to pick
his animal companion. *He dials phone.* Hello, is this the
White House? This is Morrow McCarthy. I want to cast
my vote for Fluffy. *He hangs up, says to* WALTER, *who
enters carrying a tray with tomato juice:* Does Lyssa realize
the extent to which this administration is using her? That
McDermott nomination was a total debacle. Their only

choice is to go with someone bland and unobjectionable.

JUDITH: Lyssa isn't bland and unobjectionable.

MORROW: In this town, as Senator Hughes would say, percep-
tion is everything. Focus, Judy.

JUDITH: Judith.

MORROW: This President's greatest skill is keeping himself
afloat. Why do you think he announced the nomination on
Saturday? Judith, "hello," your friend is worth a lot more
than this.

JUDITH: And this opinion has nothing to do with your new-
found commitment to the unborn?

MORROW: Don't divert the argument. It's a question of character.

JUDITH: And who would you say still does have "character"?

MORROW: The Walt Disney Company.

WALTER: Morrow just sold his screenplay to Disney for seven
figures. He started a bidding frenzy.

JUDITH: That doesn't mean they have character. That means
Morrow's mastered the art of appealing to the lowest common denominator.

MORROW: Judith, your nonpracticing heterosexuality is putting
a definite cramp in your joie de vivre.

JUDITH: Has it ever occurred to you, Morrow, that you and
many of the brightest minds in this country have been way-
laid into a simplistic position that sexual preference is the
reason for all personal and societal happiness?

MORROW: You mean it isn't?

JUDITH: There won't be national health insurance or decent
schools because of where you choose to place your penis.

MORROW: Wrong, Judith. Gay culture is penetrating the media,
theater, health, and education, and we're working on

a secret alliance with straight men for a "world without women. Amen." Aren't I right, Walter?

WALTER: I dare either of you to say any of this outside this room.

MORROW: Why are you so bitter, Judith? You're the jewel in the crown of the great society. Walter, this is another perfect example of the inconsistency of the left and the reason for my happy transition to the far right.

JUDITH: Morrow, I'm a civilian. I'm not interested in your sound bites.

MORROW: All right. If it was up to me, Judith, I'd secure both our rights to life, liberty, and the pursuit of happiness—in my case that means sleeping with men, and in your case, self-perpetuation.

JUDITH: And you don't care if you contribute to the future?

MORROW: It takes a village to contribute to the future. I'm concerned with the here and now. Does that make sense to you, Walter? You're the house intellectual.

WALTER: Absolutely.

MORROW: You're surprisingly silent this morning, Walter. No opinions on world or local news. No nominations for whose column you could have written better.

WALTER: Did you read about this Harvard professor who took hostages at the Legal Seafood Restaurant?

MORROW: Yeah, that must have been really bad clam chowder.

WALTER: I know him. We did draft counseling together. He's a brilliant guy. Very respected sociologist. Left-wing. Still listens to Ravi Shankar. Two kids. Wife's a Russian professor. He must have just totally lost it. God, that's depressing.

JUDITH: Won't happen to you, Walter. You take too many vitamins.

Voices are heard from offstage.

LYSSA: Hello! We're home! *She enters with* TIMBER TUCKER, *around forty-five, handsome, deliberately casual.*

WALTER: Hi, Lizard.

LYSSA: Hi, honey. Hi, Judith. I'm glad you're here!

MORROW: Aren't you glad I'm here?

LYSSA: Yes, but you're always here. Timber, this is my friend Dr. Judith Kaufman. Timber Tucker.

TIMBER: Dr. Hughes mentioned you during her interview this morning. She certainly admires your work.

LYSSA: And this is our friend Morrow McCarthy. Tim Tucker.

TIMBER: I miss reading your column in the *Post.*

MORROW: The President doesn't.

LYSSA: No, he's very relieved you've turned your attentions elsewhere.

MORROW: Lyssa, you're looking incandescent.

WALTER: And you, Morrow, are looking very, very taut. *To Timber:* I don't know if Lyssa mentioned me. I'm her husband, Walter Abrahmson.

LYSSA: I'm sorry.

WALTER: We were expecting you later.

LYSSA: Timber watched me shop for brunch at Dean & Deluca and followed me home. Did you get the kids to Donnie's?

WALTER: Yes, they're at Donnie's house surfing the net for messages from Iceland.

LYSSA: We're encouraging our children to become cyber-spies.

MORROW: I've been having the best time going on-line as a woman. Timber, perhaps you've seen my ad? "Single available female seeks domineering male for emasculating intrigue."

LYSSA: Walter, keep an eye out for the Senator.

TIMBER: Lyssa, is that the portrait of the General's wife that you mentioned?

LYSSA: Julia Dent Grant. Ulysses wrote her every day during the war.

WALTER: She's Lyssa's namesake. Upstairs, we have a letter from Ulysses to Julia before the battle of Vicksburg.

LYSSA: "My family is American and has been for generations in all its branches, direct and collateral."

WALTER: First line of the great "Unconditional Surrender" 's memoir.

LYSSA: Walter is very proud of *his* civil war ancestors. *She exits.*

TIMBER: Did your ancestors fight in the Civil War, Walter?

WALTER: Different civil war. The one in Minsk.

MORROW: Speaking of courage under fire, Timber, my friend Gerry got an enormous crush on you during the Gulf War. He says he'll sleep with you before Barbara Walters anytime.

TIMBER: Thank you.

LYSSA *returns.*

LYSSA: Timber caused quite a stir at Dean & Deluca.

TIMBER: Your wife is burying the lead. She also gave me a great interview this morning. I'm looking forward to following it up at brunch.

MORROW: Tell the truth, Timber. You're here for the good stuff. The ex-Mrs. Abrahmson in the basement, the runaway Chilean nanny on the fourth floor, and the joint abortion/assisted-suicide clinic in the garage. And the tawdriest of all, the real scoop on Professor Abrahmson's panel "Liberalism: Wanted Dead or Alive."

JUDITH: Walter, are you really doing something called that?

MORROW: Next Sunday night at Georgetown University.

LYSSA: Timber, let me show you where we'll be having brunch.

MORROW: I'm meeting Gerry at the gym. Timber, would you sign this copy of *The New England Journal of Medicine* for him?

TIMBER: I was hoping you'd stay for brunch. No interview, no policy talk, a sort of informal Georgetown salon with friends.

MORROW: I think you'd better ask the Abrahmsons if they'd like me to remain in their picture.

WALTER: Of course we would. Morrow's family.

MORROW: Good. 'Cause I've been waiting for a chance to tell America, "I had a threesome with Jesse and Strom in the Senate cloakroom. Hello."

TIMBER: I'd prefer you limit your insights to Dr. Hughes. I hope you'll stay too, Dr. Kaufman.

JUDITH: Sorry. I'm on call today.

LYSSA: Really? You didn't tell me that.

JUDITH: I did. Services. The higher calling.

WALTER: Lyssa, the Senator just pulled up.

LYSSA: Timber, let me show you the dining room. This is actually the oldest part of the house.

TIMBER *and* LYSSA *exit.*

WALTER: I've got to warn the Senator our guest is here already. *He exits.*

MORROW: I'll stay here and filibuster. Tell me something, Dr. Kaufman. What's wrong with heterosexual men?

JUDITH: Excuse me?

MORROW: Ever since that telegenic hunk walked in here I've been asking myself why isn't Judith B. Kaufman married. For secure men, smart women are a real turn-on. I'd have a child with you anytime. We could co-parent an amazing creation. Tell me what bank you're using and I'll make a donation.

JUDITH: How old are you, Morrow?

MORROW: Thirty. And recently worth over seven figures.

JUDITH: I don't get intimate with thirty-year-old predominantly gay men. However, you might want to meet my former husband.

MORROW: Does he like men?

JUDITH: Lumbermen. He lives in Seattle. He's a shrink who started the gay and lesbian psychiatric clinic there. He does have a friend who's an opera singer. Well, a florist who says he's an opera singer. Basically, he's a doctor's wife. Rodney keeps in shape and wears a very nice engagement ring.

MORROW: So that's why you're bitter, Dr. Kaufman.

JUDITH: Do you know how many AIDS benefits I've been to? Do you know how many donations I've made? But I am still waiting for one gay man voluntarily to come to my hospital and say, "I'm concerned about a disease that's decimating my mother, my aunts, and my sisters." My ex-husband was interviewed in the *Seattle Post* and mentioned that I was his best friend. I'm not his best friend, Morrow. I want my time back.

WALTER *reenters with* SENATOR ALAN HUGHES, *around sixty-five, and his wife,* CHARLOTTE "CHUBBY" HUGHES, *an attractive, sporty-looking woman of around sixty.*

WALTER: The boys are over at the Grahams'.

ALAN: Well, bring them by the Senate office sometime this week. Charlotte, this is my favorite other daughter, Dr. Judy. Looking good too, sweetheart. This is my favorite wife, Charlotte Hughes.

CHARLOTTE: Please call me Chubby. Everyone else does.

JUDITH: I'd slug someone who called me Chubby.

CHARLOTTE: But I never was. So it's all just amusing.

MORROW: Chubby, that's one respectable Republican cloth coat.

CHARLOTTE: I have a hat, but I left it at home.

ALAN: Morrow, how do you always manage to look younger than when I last saw you?

JUDITH: He works very hard at that, Senator.

ALAN: Walter tells me that reporter got a head start on us. How do you think Lyssa's faring with him?

MORROW: She took him brunch-shopping. That seems to have made him very happy.

CHARLOTTE: I know exactly what you mean. Sometimes I enjoy driving into Georgetown, parking the car at Dean & Deluca, and just cruising the cheese department. How can anyone be depressed when there are so many wonderful cheeses in the world?

WALTER: Would you like a drink, Alan?

CHARLOTTE: A bloody might be nice.

ALAN: Make it two bloodies.

MORROW: Three.

ALAN: Judy?

JUDITH: Too early for blood. I'll stick with apple juice.

WALTER *goes to the bar.*

MORROW: Senator Hughes, how do you feel about Lyssa's nomination?

ALAN: Do you know how goddamned great it feels to be asked about Lyssa's nomination instead of tax reform? My daughter was always a do-gooder. When she was around eight, she'd go to a birthday party and make me drop her off a block away because she didn't want anyone to feel bad because we had a nicer car. She was a candy striper in the hospital, she was on the Indian reservation for her college vacations, she was always busy starting rape centers, birthing centers, and let's-get-together-and-help-women centers. My daughter Lyssa believes that every day it's time to smile on your sister. I hope that reporter realizes how lucky this administration is to get her.

MORROW: You know, everyone who's seen Tim Tucker on *Time Zone* says he's gay as a goose.

CHARLOTTE: Impossible. He's a war reporter.

MORROW: Chubby, there are gay men who have served with distinction in the military and there are straight men who avoided the draft by dabbling in Canadian pornography, like your new son-in-law the distinguished Matlock Professor of Sociology at Georgetown.

CHARLOTTE: Walter, you never told me about any pornography!

WALTER: I did a little screenwriting to pay for my tuition in Canada.

MORROW: Chubby, next time you're at the Pleasure Chest Late Licks Video section, ask for the *Hot and Sour Strawberry Statement*—it's a counterculture classic.

The doorbell rings.

ALAN: That must be our camera crew.

MORROW: Finish making the drinks, Walter; I'll get the door.

ALAN: That boy was my brightest summer intern.

MORROW *opens front door, sees* QUINCY, *and announces:* The Prisoner of Gender!

QUINCY *enters the room.*

WALTER: Quincy!

QUINCY: Hello, Walter. I hope Lyssa didn't forget to tell you I'd be coming.

ALAN: I don't believe we've met.

WALTER: Senator, this is Quincy Quince, my former student.

MORROW: And already a best-selling author.

WALTER: You're looking at the future players here.

ALAN: This is my wife, Charlotte Hughes.

WALTER: Quincy, can I get you a drink?

QUINCY: Just water. It's nice to see you again, Dr. Kaufman. I had such fun with you and Lyssa yesterday.

JUDITH: Yes, I was hoping you'd get here a little earlier.

QUINCY: I was doing a call-in breakfast show in Maryland.

CHARLOTTE: Politics?

QUINCY: Well, politics, single-parenting, divorce, dating. The entire human agenda.

JUDITH: I'm so sorry, but I'm afraid I have to say good-bye or I'll be late for services.

CHARLOTTE: Do you go to one of those marvelous churches with a gospel choir?

WALTER: Judith is Jewish. Today is Holy Taschlich, the Festival of Regrets. "And you will cast all their sins into the depths of the sea." I was Jewish until I was bar mitzvahed. Today I am a man. I choose to be agnostic.

ALAN: Too bad more of the Senate isn't Jewish. It would be bumper to bumper all the way to the Potomac.

QUINCY: Someday I'd love to talk to you about being black and Jewish. You're a walking Crown Heights.

JUDITH *exits.*

MORROW: I think she's an incredibly sexy woman.

WALTER: You find cosmic anger sexy?

MORROW: Why shouldn't she be angry? As far as she's concerned, there's only one way to save the world and people like me are screwing it up. In fact, I'm the worst kind of offender: gay, conservative, and total media hype.

QUINCY: I enjoy the media. I always have a good time.

ALAN: There's a healthy attitude. Maybe Quincy here's the one who should run for office.

QUINCY: No, sir. I have two more books to write and I want to start my family before I focus on my public life. My generation wants to do it all, but we want to have some fun too. Don't you think sex is wildly important, Walter?

WALTER: Sex is important. Sure.

ALAN: Wildly.

QUINCY: My next book is about women restoring their sexual identity. It's called *Venus Raging*. Sex for Lyssa's generation became just something else to be good at. Like weight lifting. We, on the other hand, want to come home to a warm penis.

MORROW: Walter, this woman is a visionary.

LYSSA *reenters with* TIMBER.

LYSSA: Hello, Charlotte. You're looking very well. Marriage suits you.

CHARLOTTE: We had a wonderful time.

LYSSA: Hello, Dad.

ALAN: Hello, Mousey.

QUINCY: Mousey?

ALAN: She was a mouse in the *Nutcracker* when she was six.

TIMBER: I bet you never called your son Mouse.

ALAN: No. We would have called him Rat King. You must be Timber Tucker. A good reporter can't resist an obvious remark.

"My generation wants to do it all, but we want to have some fun
too. Don't you think sex is wildly important, Walter?"
(Peter Riegert, Hal Holbrook, Elizabeth Marvel)

LYSSA: Timber, doesn't my dad have a great handshake? When I was eight and he first ran for mayor of Fort Wayne, my dad taught me how to shake hands. "Firm; not like a lady, not like a man. Just shoot from the hip."

ALAN: Look 'em straight in the eye.

QUINCY: Timber, I'm Quincy Quince. I was very moved by your report on the women of Sarajevo. I thought it was really terrific.

MORROW: Lyssa, we've been having a heated debate over the role of religion and sex in a secular society.

QUINCY: Senator, how much do your religious beliefs account for your antichoice position on abortion?

ALAN: Miss Quince—I love saying your name, Miss Quince— I like to think that my beliefs account for an open dialogue.

LYSSA: Dad, your beliefs on this subject are untenable. How can you be so adamant about individual rights, and deny the most personal right, when and if to have child?

MORROW: All life, physical or intellectual, begins at conception.

LYSSA: How would you know?

MORROW: Lyssa, you want to treat religion as random predjudice. But, in fact, my morality is based on logic. There is increasing evidence that who we are as human beings is determined by genetic structure. We've even dicovered that in sexual preference. Therefore, I draw the line at conception. Where do you draw the line, Senator?

ALAN: "But Mary kept all these things and pondered them in her heart." Luke 2:19.

LYSSA: In times of conflict, my father always quotes the Bible. Is anyone hungry? I'll see how Carmelita's doing with that brunch.

TIMBER: Is Carmelita your nanny, Dr. Hughes?

LYSSA: No. Carmelita is our housekeeper and her Social Security is fully paid.

QUINCY: Lyssa, don't you think that the entire nannygate incident was an outgrowth of the seventies' having-it-all mythology?

TIMBER: Dr. Hughes, are you home when your kids get in from school?

LYSSA: Timber, would *you* be home when your kids got in from school?

TIMBER: No, I'd be in Rwanda. But my wife would be home.

WALTER: Are you kidding? If she worked, she'd be out with a client; if she didn't work, she'd be out with her trainer or driving the kids to gymnastics. Most women I know are booked solid from morning till night. For instance . . .

LYSSA: Walter thinks I'm slightly hysterical because I am overcommitted and determined to do everything well.

WALTER: For instance, it used to be whenever Lyssa was called for jury duty, she inevitably had to be out of town lecturing that day or at a world conference for gonorrhea.

MORROW: Who's hosting?

WALTER: Although a phone call to postpone would have sufficed, she would drag herself to the court bearing the full range of excuses: plane ticket, lecture schedule, and a case study of the feasibility of HMOs for any interested bureaucrat.

LYSSA: Walter, you're exaggerating. I did that once.

CHARLOTTE: I didn't even know doctors had to serve on a jury.

WALTER: The final notice arrived on a day when both boys had the chicken pox, our nanny disappeared, to elope with the neighborhood drug-dealing security guard, and there was a crisis at the hospital only Lyssa could solve. So I advised her not even to open it. No professional woman of her class does. They're all too goddamn busy!

LYSSA: Walter, I didn't deliberately not open it. I just misplaced it.

WALTER: And you know what's so great about the American justice system? I was right. She never heard from them again.

ALAN: My daughter has always been a hard worker, and, believe me, I know what hard work is. I grew up on a farm in Indiana. Miss Quince, I'd like to hear more about *Venus Raging*. Sounds like a pretty good country western song to me. *He begins singing:*

> "Oh, she's mashing her potatoes,
> but Venus is Raging just for me!"

LYSSA: Dad!

ALAN: Imagine the humiliation this poor girl has suffered having me as her father.

MORROW: This is gold, Timber. Pure gold. Call your segment on Lyssa "An American Daughter." It's another Emmy in the bag for you.

ALAN: How 'bout that brunch, Lyssa?

CHARLOTTE: I like to call it *petit déjeuner*.

ALAN: Let's show our reporter how real Washingtonians eat. Come along, young Morrow. Tell Timber how gay culture will redefine the Midwest.

MORROW: Have you been to Cincinnati recently, sir? One out of ten Republicans there is gay.

ALAN: That explains why the Cincinnati airport is in Kentucky. Transport homophobia.

LYSSA: If anyone's interested, we're eating now.

ALAN: Walter, would you put some nice music into the dining room and bring in another pitcher of bloodies?

LYSSA: Timber, has my father told you that, just like our famous ancestor, we rely on stimulants.

CHARLOTTE: And bring in some fizzy water. We want fizzy water.

All exit except WALTER *and* QUINCY.

QUINCY: I'll help you carry it in.

WALTER: How do you like your bloodies, Quincy? Mary, Virgin, Typhoid?

QUINCY: I don't think your wife likes me.

WALTER: I thought all women like you.

QUINCY: I'm too happy for all women to like me.

WALTER: Are you saying my wife isn't happy?

QUINCY: I can't find her soul.

WALTER: You've only just met her.

QUINCY: I've become very spiritual.

WALTER: I don't connect to this current craze for spirituality.

QUINCY: People are searching for meaning now.

WALTER: You mean they never have before? How, then, do you explain Chartres?

QUINCY: You're so brilliant, Walter.

WALTER: Easy assessment. You've been on too many human-agenda call-in shows. I, on the other hand, have been biding my time.

QUINCY: Are you kidding? *Towards a Lesser Elite* is practically a classic now. Everyone at the Renaissance Weekend said it's like the blueprint for deconstructing liberalism.

WALTER: You went to one of those weekends? Who was there?

QUINCY: Well, I mean, like everybody. Walter, aren't they waiting for their Bloody Marys?

WALTER: I want to know who was "like" at this Renaissance Weekend.

QUINCY: Well, some *New Republic* people, some academics, some policy wonks, and some up-and-coming Northwest info-highway types.

WALTER: And who, like, was the most impressive "type"?

QUINCY: I don't know. Maybe Teddy Kenwright.

WALTER: Oh. Him.

QUINCY: Walter, while you guys saw never-ending opportunities for women, gays, and blacks, Teddy Kenwright called the opposite. He's a real player now.

WALTER: He's not a player like you. According to *Time* magazine, you're one of our fifty top leaders under thirty.

QUINCY: You saw that?

WALTER: According to *Time*, you're bringing feminism into the twenty-first century. Has it ever occurred to you that maybe it should cease and desist in the twentieth century, like Soviet communism or the rotary dial.

QUINCY: You don't believe that.

WALTER: You just said my wife isn't happy, and according to *Time*, she's one of our fifty top leaders over forty. I was on the waiting list.

QUINCY: I said I couldn't find her soul.

WALTER: Do you mean she's not sexy?

QUINCY: Walter, I don't want to get into this with you. You are one of my all-time heroes.

WALTER: You think my wife is one of those seventies good girls who came to prominence in the nineties and schedules half an hour a day for spontaneity.

QUINCY: Do you want to kiss me, Walter? 'Cause I think you've wanted to kiss me all these years. Is that what this is about?

WALTER: Is it?

QUINCY: Walter, you spend too much time in your head. Just
  kiss me, 'cause it's no big deal.

WALTER: Did Teddy Kenwright kiss you at the Renaissance
  Weekend?

QUINCY: No. I let him goose me under the table during the
  Ethics in Society panel.

WALTER: You still haven't told me if you like your Bloody
  Virgin or Mary.

QUINCY: Have I shocked you?

WALTER: No. But Teddy Kenwright is minor-league talent.

QUINCY: In all departments.

WALTER: And you're wrong about my wife. She's a very happy
  woman.

QUINCY: Are you happy, Walter?

WALTER: Me?

QUINCY: You.

WALTER: I live in one of the nicest homes in Georgetown. My
  wife is Ulysses S. Grant's fifth-generation granddaughter.
  My children are both at the Sidwell Friends School and
  floating through cyberspace, and my five-year-old book is
  a standard for deconstructing liberalism. Am I happy,
  Quincy Quince? I want a Bloody Mary. Okay with you?

QUINCY: Fine. Walter, I'm scared of going in there.

WALTER: Don't be ridiculous.

QUINCY: I can tell Morrow thinks I'm like virtual stupidity.

WALTER: So what. Morrow thinks I'm like actual stupidity.
  That's Morrow's job.

QUINCY: I love it when you laugh. You're such a kind man,
  Walter.

WALTER: Do you like the Beach Boys?

QUINCY: Surf City, there you go.

WALTER: That's Jan and Dean. The Beach Boys are Help me,
  Rhonda.

QUINCY: All that California crap is so limited in positive body
  imagery for women.
WALTER: Fine. No Beach Boys. Wilson Pickett it is. *He puts*
  on the music and begins dancing with QUINCY. *He kisses*
  her as LYSSA *walks into the room.*
LYSSA: Walter, can you bring Chubby the fizzy water? And
  Daddy says he prefers Mozart to Wilson Pickett. *She exits.*
WALTER: Quincy, would you carry the fizzy water for Chubby?
  Chubby likes her water fizzy.

Later that afternoon. TIMBER *is seated to the side with* JIMMY, *a cameraman.* SENATOR HUGHES, MORROW, CHARLOTTE, WALTER, *and* QUINCY *are informally seated.* LYSSA *is serving coffee.*

ALAN:

> "Off to the west, in Memphis, where the sun's
> Mid-morning fire beat on a wider stream.
> His purpose headstrong as a river runs,
> Grant closed a smoky door on aides and guards
> And chewed through scheme on scheme
> For toppling Vicksburg like a house of cards."

And the poet is? Can you take it, Harvard?

WALTER: Carl Sandburg.

ALAN: Sorry. For twenty points, can you take it, Princeton?

MORROW: Walt Whitman.

ALAN: No. Time's up. The answer is Richard Wilbur. Perhaps we still need to fund arts education, gentlemen. Quality of life. It's an issue of quality of life.

LYSSA: Coffee, Dad?

WALTER: That was a great brunch, Lizard. Unbelievably good!

LYSSA: Carmelita.

WALTER: Don't give all the credit to Carmelita, honey.

LYSSA: Why not? You were certainly occupied elsewhere.

CHARLOTTE: Lyssa, darling, these madeleines are scrumptious.

LYSSA: They're just "Lite" vanilla wafers from a box. Our boys like them.

MORROW: All "lite" references are really euphemisms for gay. Therefore, the expression "He's a little lite in the loafers."

QUINCY: I've never heard that.

MORROW: Then you also wouldn't know that "Lite" potato chips and cream cheese are officially approved gay products.

LYSSA: Timber, maybe we should do this another time. My family is getting tired.

ALAN: Nonsense, Mousey, we're all here now and having a great time!

TIMBER: We'll only use a minute of this. You're all doing great.

CHARLOTTE: Lyssa, you have nothing to worry about. You are the epitome of good breeding. You're so calm and collected.

LYSSA: Actually, I'm a person who always feels compelled to make an effort. I've always envied grace under pressure.

CHARLOTTE: Oh, me too. Timber, I'm not a quote-unquote feminist. But I was the first female manager of the Southampton Golf Club and the first to host the Dinah Shore Classic.

ALAN: Lyssa's mother was a great fan of Dinah Shore's! She wanted to see the U.S.A. in a Chevrolet.

LYSSA: I don't remember my mother having any sense of adventure at all. She was the kind of ordinary Indiana housewife who took pride in her icebox cakes and cheese pimento canapés.

TIMBER: Icebox cakes? I'm sorry, what are icebox cakes?

LYSSA: They were a sort of Mount Saint Helen's that erupted overnight in the refrigerator. You alternate layers of cookies and whipped cream and then chill.

ALAN: She was a terrific woman. Unfortunately, Lyssa lost her when she was only fourteen.

MORROW: That must have been very difficult.

LYSSA: As I get older I regret not having known her better. But I wasn't particularly close to her at the time. And Dad sent me east to boarding school that year, so I didn't really suffer.

ALAN: I think my daughter has tremendous reserves of strength and compassion. Maybe it is because she lost her mother at such a young age. I believe Lyssa is about as close to a female role model as we get.

MORROW: Hear, hear! If I had to vote for the person I thought had genuine confidence and class, it would be Lyssa.

LYSSA: Okay, Morrow. You can stay for supper.

MORROW: No, it's true. With your nomination, another political dynasty, like the Roosevelts or the Kennedys, is being established. Americans always enshrine their elite.

WALTER: I have to disagree. The future vitality of this country is not coming from traditional sources but from a diverse multicultural wellspring.

MORROW: But who's still in charge, Walter? Hello! It's not a common story that the Asian gay president of the United States turns to his African-American disabled lesbian vice president and says we have to be sure to have at least one straight white guy in the Cabinet. Let's give him Transportation.

LYSSA: Morrow, I would say that anyone who dined through Princeton at the Ivy Club, wrote a column for the *Washington Post*, and just sold a movie for a million dollars is far more elitist than individuals from families with a tradition of public service.

MORROW: I am an elitist. I have to be. I represent a persecuted minority. That's absolutely true. But what's far more insidious is the current left-wing rage for selective privilege or self-righteous entitlement. Am I right, Senator?

ALAN: Morrow, I lost you at the gay cream cheese.

MORROW: I'm making a legitimate point here. There are liberal professionals who believe they deserve special treatment because their heart is in the right place. For example, your daughter and my best friend, Dr. Lyssa Dent Hughes, Surgeon General nominee, a woman of impeccable commitment, at the forefront of women's health issues, pro-choice, pro-gay, has never served on a jury.

LYSSA: I ...

CHARLOTTE: Well, she's a very busy woman.

ALAN: Have you ever served on a jury, Morrow?

MORROW: I'm not a registered voter. I'm still technically Canadian.

LYSSA: I've always had work and family conflicts when the invitations arrived. I mean summonses.

ALAN: A person has two choices, Morrow. You can either shoot the cattle or run for Congress. Old family homily.

MORROW: I don't follow, sir.

ALAN: Well, it makes about as much sense as your theory about selective privilege.

MORROW: Well, wait ... wait. Are you saying that the people who do answer their "invitations," who do serve on juries, are less crucial to their family and work than your daughter? Not everyone can believe that their innate goodness, their superior agenda, simply gives them the right to ignore the invitation.

LYSSA: I always presented my conflicts to the court.

MORROW: Except for the time when you didn't.

CHARLOTTE: I once didn't pay a parking ticket and nothing ever happened.

ALAN: My daughter has been a diligent and brilliant public health administrator. She will be a brilliant and diligent Surgeon General. *He gets up and shakes Timber's hand.* Thank you, Timber. This has been terrific fun. I'm sorry, but Chubby and I are expected at another brunch. That's the great thing about brunch: it goes on all day.

TIMBER: Thank you, sir. I appreciate your time. Dr. Hughes, I'm sorry, I have to ask you something, just for clarification. *He signals for* JIMMY *to move in with the camera.* Did you deliberately not answer the jury-duty notification?

LYSSA: No. I believe I misplaced it.

TIMBER: Subsequently, did you contact the County Clerk's office?

LYSSA: No.

TIMBER: Were you intending to bring this up at your confirmation hearing?

LYSSA: It didn't occur to me.

WALTER: Timber, my wife is a mother of two small children. She is a professor of public health at Georgetown and ran a major public hospital. Not to mention a nationally known lecturer. She is, in fact, a very busy woman.

ALAN: Lyssa, please walk us to the car.

TIMBER: Senator, do you believe your colleagues who share your antichoice position on abortion will seize on this information to embarrass the President's second nominee?

ALAN: Timber, now let me ask you something. "Who's buried in Grant's tomb?" The answer is about as interesting as what my daughter did with a piece of paper. I think most Americans would rather know more about my beautiful fourth wife. I fell in love with her when I found out her name was Chubby. Good-bye.

ALAN, CHARLOTTE, *and* LYSSA *exit.*

QUINCY: There's another way to look at this "Lyssa Dent Hughes Problem." Dr. Hughes is a prisoner of her gender. She took on so many obligations that the basic necessities of life, like responding to a simple jury form, became overwhelming. The best intentions in females often become the seeds of their own destruction.

TIMBER: Okay. We have it. Thanks. Dr. Abrahmson, do you mind if I go upstairs and get some footage of the letter from Vicksburg?

WALTER: Help yourself.

QUINCY: May I join you? I'm fascinated by homes. This is a uniquely historical but lived-in one.

QUINCY, TIMBER, *and* JIMMY *exit.*

MORROW: That woman is a moron.

WALTER: Why the fuck did you do that?

MORROW: I didn't do anything. He's the one who's making a meal out of this. He's just the kind of heterosexual man I can't bear.

WALTER: But you brought up the jury-duty notice.

MORROW: Then you should have protected Lyssa and not mentioned it to begin with. You put it out there, Walter. If I hadn't caught it, imagine where Miss Warm Penis would have run with it. I just saved you, Walter. You should be grateful to me.

WALTER: Do you hate us all because we're straight?

"I didn't do anything. He's the one who's making a meal out of this.
He's just the kind of heterosexual man I can't bear."
(Bruce Norris, Cotter Smith)

MORROW: Only a straight man would be insensitive enough to ask that question.

LYSSA *comes back in.*

LYSSA: Daddy says he'll call us later.
MORROW: I thought your father gave a vintage performance. And I've got a secret yen for Chubby.
LYSSA: Isn't Gerry waiting for you at the gym, Morrow?
MORROW: Don't waste your time being upset about this, Lyssa. The more Timber's show is talked about, the greater the buzz for you. Why can't you just see it all as a game? I love you, Lyssa. You'll never know how important you are to me.
LYSSA: Good-bye, Morrow.

MORROW *exits.*

WALTER: Don't worry, Lizard, everything's going to be fine. Your father's right. No one's interested. There are survivalist Nazis overturning the government in Idaho.
LYSSA: They haven't been nominated for Surgeon General.
WALTER: We can spin you right out of this. I'll call my old roommate Ted Kramer at the *Times.*
LYSSA: I'm very tired, Walter. Why don't you take Quincy home?
WALTER: I don't want to take Quincy home. She can take a taxi. I want to be with you.
LYSSA: I'd feel better if you took her home.
WALTER: So then you could not speak to me for a week and tell me two months later it was because I took fucking Quincy home.
LYSSA: Fucking Quincy. You know, that's what girls of her

generation enjoy doing, as opposed to the frigid, over-extended no-fun narcissists of my generation. Isn't that why you kissed her?

WALTER: It just happened. It didn't mean anything.

LYSSA: In our house, it happened in our house.

QUINCY *and* TIMBER *reenter the room.* JIMMY *exits the house.*

QUINCY: I loved the letter from Vicksburg. It's very poignant. For a soldier, he had great depth. I can't imagine what it is to literally fight for one's principles.

LYSSA: Quincy, Walter said he'd drive you home.

QUINCY: I'm just at the Four Seasons. I can take a cab.

LYSSA: Georgetown isn't as safe as it used to be. Thank you for coming. Walter has always been so proud of your achievements. Where we erred you will surely transcend

WALTER *exits.*

QUINCY: Good-bye, Timber. I'll send you the book. *She exits.*

TIMBER: I didn't think you'd be capable of it.

LYSSA: What?

TIMBER: Pettiness.

LYSSA: That wasn't petty. It was out-and-out bitterness combined with envy and competition. I'm baiting my husband. Give me a little credit here, Mr. Lawn.

TIMBER: Who's Mr. Lawn?

LYSSA: You. Forest Lawn. Piney Tucker, Timbarton Oaks, Timber Canoe and Tyler too. Frankly, of all of us, Chubby is my favorite. At least she's genuine.

TIMBER: I think you're pretty genuine. And I specialize in sizing up people in fifty-second segments.

LYSSA: Can you not use it?

TIMBER: Are you asking me if I can ignore information I wish I didn't have?

LYSSA: No.

TIMBER: It's my job. Sometimes I wish it wasn't. I'd rather be covering the fanatic at Legal Seafood. It's clearer. But they'll probably use this tonight.

LYSSA: Will it be bad for my father?

TIMBER: Yes, but he's a veteran, he can handle it. I'm sorry I had to ask you those questions. I assumed you'd be ready with the answer.

LYSSA: Maybe Quincy has all the answers. Are you attracted to her?

TIMBER: Way too old. I'm into twenty-year-old bimbos. You with me?

LYSSA: Girls in swimsuits on the cover of *Sports Illustrated*.

TIMBER: I should title your segment "An American Snob." Swimsuit girls are much too upscale. I'm talkin' Dunkin' Donuts twins in Eugene. The cashier at the Shreveport airport. That's America to me. Ba-dabing, ba-da-boom. She gets you a beer and turns into a sandwich.

LYSSA: What kind of a sandwich?

TIMBER: Are you really choosing to continue this conversation with me?

LYSSA: Right now, my husband probably has his hand up Quincy's Quince, I've probably just set back the case for every cause I believe in, not to mention cast a dark shadow on women in government, and put the final lid on national health insurance. So, yes, I really do want to know what kind of fucking sandwich.

TIMBER: Brie with pesto and sun-dried tomatoes.

LYSSA: What a pretentious sandwich! She couldn't turn into a tuna!

The doorbell rings.

LYSSA: Maybe it's Quincy. She's finished another book.
TIMBER: You're much more tart than I expected.
LYSSA: You two think alike. She told me exactly the same thing.

JUDITH *enters, sopping wet.*

JUDITH: It's Elijah. I'm wet and I'm early.
LYSSA: Is it raining? Why are you wet?
JUDITH: A puddle. I was walking on M Street. Al Gore's dog
    jumped into a puddle and splashed me.
TIMBER: How do you know it was Al Gore's dog?
JUDITH: All right. It was Colin Powell's dog. He was showering
    me with sisterly love.
LYSSA: Judith, there's a robe in the laundry room. Why don't
    you change?

JUDITH *exits.*

TIMBER: Is she okay?
LYSSA: I don't know.
TIMBER: My, my, lady, you've had a day!
LYSSA: Yes. It's been fun, fun, fun, till my T-bird came. Walter
    likes the Beach Boys. Good-bye, Timber.
TIMBER: Dr. Hughes, I can't stop what's coming down the
    pike. Thank God, I'm not that powerful. But, I'd like to
    try and guide you through this.
LYSSA: Like a Boy Scout?
TIMBER: Like a friend. It all depends on how you play it. I'd
    say don't shoot the cattle yet. Keep running for Congress.

JUDITH *reenters.*

LYSSA: Better?

JUDITH: Better.

LYSSA: Good-bye, Timber.

TIMBER: You can reach me at this number. I'd like to help you. Remember, grace under pressure. *He exits.*

LYSSA: Do you want a cup of tea?

JUDITH: Why does he want to help you?

LYSSA: Our post-brunch show didn't go very well. Morrow was a real shit. And Walter behaved like a teenager.

JUDITH: Sounds like business as usual.

LYSSA: No. This was worse. I may be in some trouble.

JUDITH: I tried to drown myself, Lyssa.

LYSSA: What?

JUDITH: I went to the Festival of Regrets. I prayed by the banks of the Potomac. There were old men davening in prayer shawls, and young lawyers in Brooks Brothers suits. I watched while the men tossed in their breadcrumbs of secret sorrow. "Oh, Lord, my God, I cheated on my income tax." "Oh, Lord, King of the universe, I lust for the Asian checkout girl at Hany Farms delicatessen." "Oh, Lord, I have sinned, I dreamt about a strip of bacon." At first I remained silent. I stood there feeling my familiar distance and disdain. And then, almost involuntarily, I began shredding my low-fat cranberry-orange muffin. I wanted this God, this Yaveh, to know me. So I tossed my first crumb into the water. "Oh, Lord, my God, King of the universe, I have failed to honor my mother and father," and that regret floats out to Maryland. "Oh, Lord, my God, I distrust most people I know, I feel no comfort in their happiness, no sympathy for their sorrow." A tiny cranberry sits still upon the water. "Oh, Lord, our God, who is like you in Earth or in Heaven, I regret the men I've been with, I regret the marriage I made, I regret never having children,

I regret never having learned to be a woman." I pull off the entire top and a wad of muffin sails like a frigate towards the Washington Monument. "Oh, Lord, my God, Mighty of Mighty, Holy of Holy, I can't make life and I can't stop death. Oh, Lord, my God, the Lord is one, I've wasted my life," and I jump in.

LYSSA: And then.

JUDITH: It seems I'm still a very good swimmer.

LYSSA: Yes, I remember. Freshman phys ed.

JUDITH: The Potomac isn't very cold in September. It's still warm from the summer lights.

LYSSA: So you were fine.

JUDITH: I was great. I was bobbing up and down in my pearls and Liz Claiborne suit, when I noticed a box of Dunkin' Donut holes floating along. And suddenly I remembered the slogan from my mother's favorite donut shop, "As you ramble on through life, whatever be your goal, keep your eye upon the donut, and not upon the hole." And I began laughing and laughing. Now I had a purpose. Now I had a goal. I must rescue the donut holes and bring them here to you on N Street. Lyssa, these are the donut holes of my discontent!

LYSSA: Thank you.

JUDITH: Of course no taxi would stop for a drenched black woman who just crawled out of the Potomac. So I walked all the way.

LYSSA: Well, I'm glad you're feeling better. *She starts upstairs.*

JUDITH: Where are you going?

LYSSA: Upstairs. I need to call my children.

JUDITH: They're fine. Please. Lyssa, I'm so cold! And I'm so sad!

LYSSA: Do you ever think that other people might have their own fears, their own sorrow?

JUDITH: I spend my life trying to relieve other people's pain and sorrow. I want a home.

LYSSA: God damn it, Judith! Then just grow up and make one.

JUDITH: I can't. Not just for me.

LYSSA: I'm sorry. I can't help you tonight.

JUDITH: You don't know what it is to want, Lyssa.

LYSSA: What gives you the audacity to believe you've failed if you can't make life or stop death?

JUDITH: Because I was taught if I was a good girl and worked hard I could.

LYSSA: Good-bye, Judith.

LYSSA *exits.* JUDITH *looks at the portrait of Julia Grant.*

JUDITH: Happy New Year, Julia. *La Shana Tovah.*

After a moment, LYSSA *reappears.*

JUDITH: Happy New Year, Lyssa.

LYSSA: Happy New Year, Judith.

ACT TWO

Saturday afternoon, a week later. WALTER *is smoking and reading the morning paper. At least six other newspapers and magazines are on the floor.* LYSSA *is peeking through the closed blinds of the window.*

LYSSA: Walter, another television van just pulled up! Don't they have an election or a revolution to cover?

WALTER: It's all about the goddamn pimentos!

LYSSA: What?

WALTER: The cheese pimento canapés. You have single-handedly proven that no one in this country really gives a fuck about the jury system but they care an awful lot about the "ordinary" Indiana housewives who take pride in their "icebox cakes and cheese pimento canapés."

LYSSA: Oh, God, it's that girl with the teeth from the five o'clock news team.

WALTER: Are you listening?

LYSSA: What?

WALTER: *USA Today* says the housewives of Indiana are picketing the radio stations. The "icebox cakes and cheese pimento canapé" moms are apparently furious with you for

"minimizing their lives." The boys even found a fuckin'
"Ladies Chat Room" about you on the NET.

LYSSA: Jesus, another van.

WALTER: Of course. In a fucking week you've gone from being
a compromise candidate to the fucking soccer moms' anti-
Christ.

LYSSA: Walter, can you please try to talk to me without saying
"fuck" or chain-smoking?

WALTER: You're so goddamn prissy.

Telephone rings.

LYSSA: I'm not answering that.

Telephone rings again. They wait.

WALTER: Maybe it's the President.

Telephone rings again.

LYSSA *on the phone:* Hello. No. No, Martha, I didn't know.
Thank you. *She hangs up.* I've made the cover of the *New
York Post.* There's a picture of me at Safeway yesterday
and a headline: "DR. ICEBOX SHOPS."

WALTER: I told you, Lizard, you've created a female sound bite
on a fucking par with "I am not a crook" and George
Romney being brainwashed.

LYSSA: If you didn't read six newspapers every morning, you
wouldn't have to know all of this.

WALTER: You're my wife. Of course I have to know all of this.
You can't go back on *Time Zone* without knowing what's
been said about you. Did you read Quincy's op-ed in the
Post this morning?

LYSSA: Yes. And I saw her on *Nightline, Equal Time, Crossfire,* and weekend *Good Morning America.* My nomination is going to sell Quincy a hell of a lot of books. They'll be taking prisoners of gender across America.

WALTER: I thought her op-ed was very sympathetic.

LYSSA: Fuck off, Walter.

WALTER: No, really, Lizard. She was right. You're "being repositioned by the media as a victim feminist, which absurdly undermines your legitimacy as a power one."

LYSSA: Please don't quote Quincy to me.

The phone rings again.

LYSSA: It's probably *Penthouse!*

The phone rings again.

WALTER *calls offstage:* Carmelita! Can you take the calls?

The phone stops ringing.

WALTER: Honey, we can fix this. This is not the time to be stubborn.

LYSSA: I'm not being stubborn. I know what I'm doing. I'm going to tell the truth.

WALTER: Fine. Great. Then you have to be able to handle it.

LYSSA: I can handle it. I will drag myself in front of every Congress person, every newspaper reporter, and every talk-show host in the country. I will appear daily for the Senate hearings. I will tell Timber Tucker that what's happening is wrong. Here's a person who can do some good, who has done a lot of good, and a goddamn misplaced slip of paper is being used to unravel all her possibilities. That's unacceptable.

WALTER: It isn't just a person, Lyssa. It's you.

LYSSA: I know that.

WALTER: No, you don't. This has nothing to do with the goddamn slip of paper. It doesn't even have anything to do with your politics. It's the women of America who are furious with you, Lizard. You're pretty, you have two great kids, you're successful, you're admired, you're thin, and you have a great soul. Face it, Lizard, in the heartland that means you're one prissy privileged ungrateful-to-her-mother, conniving bitch.

LYSSA: So now I have to ingratiate myself with the housewives of Indiana?

WALTER: Trust me on this. I'm still a pretty decent sociologist even if I haven't written anything good in five years.

LYSSA: Oh, God, Walter, everyone knows you're brilliant.

WALTER: Please, Lyssa, stop being Miss M.D.-Ph.D., holier than thou, with God on my side, give me your tired, your poor, I speak for all women fucking role models.

ALAN *and* CHARLOTTE *enter, with a young man, around twenty-eight,* BILLY ROBBINS, *who wears a blue blazer, chinos, and sparkling clear glasses.*

ALAN: Is this the home of a woman who hates icebox cakes and her mother?

LYSSA: You left out children and polio victims. I hate them too. Hi, Dad. Hello, Charlotte.

CHARLOTTE: Hello, darling. Lyssa, you look tired. Call my Eva at Elizabeth Arden's. She'll take care of you.

ALAN: Have you heard from the President?

LYSSA: No.

ALAN: This is Billy Robbins from my office.

LYSSA: Hello.

BILLY: Hello.

ALAN: He's the best spin-control man in the Senate. And he's only twelve.

BILLY: Your dad invited me along with him today. I hope you don't mind.

CHARLOTTE: How can you bear having all those reporters camping out on your doorstep?

BILLY: Call me before you say anything to them. Even hello.

LYSSA: I'll just change their water daily.

WALTER: I told Lyssa all she needs is a strategy. And she'll believe a stranger before she believes me.

BILLY: Professor, I wrote a paper on your book for poly sci sophomore year at Berkeley. It's amazing how quickly popular opinions change. Dr. Hughes, your father told me Tim Tucker's doing a follow-up interview tomorrow. Word is Barbara and Diane can't believe he nabbed you from under them. The Lyssa Hughes interview is a real get.

LYSSA: What's a "get"?

CHARLOTTE: Like shopping, dear. Something you're just dying to get.

ALAN: Lyssa's best friend has also asked to speak with Timber.

BILLY: Who's that?

WALTER: A crazy lady.

ALAN: Dr. Judith B. Kaufman. Lyssa's known her since Miss Porter's.

BILLY: I wouldn't play up the Miss Porter's bit. Too elitist. Doesn't that school have another name?

LYSSA: Farmington.

BILLY: Fine. Tell her to say you met at Farmington High.

LYSSA: Judith was the first African American on full scholarship.

BILLY: Affirmative action. Also dicey.

LYSSA: All right. She was the first Jew on full scholarship.

BILLY: I just want to present you in the best possible light. You may be a privileged person but you're also a working mom, you love your husband, you love your kids, you've got great family values, and on Sunday you go to church and enjoy hiking.

LYSSA: Do I also coach the gymnastics team?

BILLY: I wish you did.

WALTER: Lyssa's being sarcastic.

BILLY: No sarcasm admitted. Nothing East Coast, Ivy League, smarty-pants, no women's lib, no highfallutin charm. Remember, you're from Indiana.

LYSSA: I haven't lived in Indiana in thirty years.

BILLY: Your father's the senator from Indiana. He was the mayor of Fort Wayne.

LYSSA: Uh-huh.

CHARLOTTE: I thought I'd hate Indianapolis, but it's really rather charming. And there's that enchanting little Speedway restaurant.

BILLY: Basically, Americans will forgive a wife who, with the help of her loving family, overcomes a personal deficiency.

ALAN: My daughter has no deficiencies.

BILLY: Simple people who aren't great-granddaughters of Presidents and PhDs in public health serve on a jury when they receive an official notice.

WALTER: Mr. Robbins is right, Lizard.

BILLY: Sometimes it's just a question of knowing what the people want and giving it to them and then get on with it.

LYSSA: I can't pretend to be someone I'm not.

BILLY: I don't agree with your politics, Dr. Hughes, but I have the greatest respect for you and Professor Abrahmson. You've gotten yourself into a mess and I'd like to try to get you out of it. Now can I see the room where Timber will be conducting the interview.

LYSSA: This is it.

BILLY: Maybe we should do it in the kitchen. It's a little more homey.

LYSSA: Or we could do it in the laundry. I could be folding.

WALTER: Let's look at the kitchen.

ALAN *putting his arm around* BILLY: C'mon, Mr. Robbins. Remind me to show you the famous letter from Vicksburg.

BILLY: By the way, I'd focus on Grant the General and not Grant the President. Someone's likely to bring up whiskey fraud and corruption.

LYSSA: That was more than a hundred years ago.

BILLY: We don't want them to be reminded. In the latest CNN/*Washington Post* ranking of the U.S. Presidents, Grant came in forty-first, just above last-place Warren Harding. Morrow McCarthy mentioned that on Charlie Rose last night. Charlie got a three share when Morrow was on, which is very impressive for Charlie.

LYSSA: Well, I'm glad I could help.

BILLY: Morrow's a real crossover talent. We're lucky he's been publicly very supportive of you.

BILLY, ALAN, *and* WALTER *exit.*

CHARLOTTE: Do you think that man ever has sex?

LYSSA: Excuse me?

CHARLOTTE: Do you think that immaculate little man ever takes off those preppie little clothes and gets down and dirty and a little nasty-sweaty? Scary perma-pressed creature. *She takes out a cigarette, a cigarette holder, and a gold lighter.* Do you mind if I smoke? Oh, God, of course you do. I won't light it. I only started up again last month

to celebrate the twentieth anniversary of my quitting. So
how are you with all of this?

LYSSA: I'm going to fight it, in my own way.

Phone rings twice.

CHARLOTTE: Isn't the President an old friend of yours?

LYSSA: I went to Bryn Mawr with his wife. And two of Walter's
classmates are in the Cabinet. But Walter isn't speaking to
either of them.

CHARLOTTE: Whatever. My point is you're the President's
nominee and you're his wife's personal friend. It's his responsibility to defend you. Especially because he is the
same party as you, and your father is not.

LYSSA: I never asked for my father to defend me.

CHARLOTTE: You're lucky you never had to. Your father's getting at least two thousand calls a day. He's torn. He's a
very good father but he's also a very good Senator. And
he'll be up for reelection.

LYSSA: I know, but what can I do?

CHARLOTTE: Let me give you some advice. I know what it is
to be out there on a limb. I raised two boys alone before
it was chic or even admirable. Protect your family, protect
your marriage, and if you don't, I certainly will protect
mine. There are plenty of not-nice people in the world,
Lyssa. They'll tear you apart just because they're jealous
or disappointed or, even worse, because they have nothing
better to do. Then, after it's all over, after all the damage
and the hurt is done, you come back to yourself. So you
can ruin your life by being valiant and impressive or find
the most idiotic means to move forward gracefully.
Frankly, that's why until I married your father I took two

"There are plenty of not-nice people in the world, Lyssa. They'll tear you apart just because they're jealous or disappointed or, even worse, because they have nothing better to do."

(Kate Nelligan, Penny Fuller)

Anacins every morning for thirty years. I never expected to
be this happy, especially in the derriere of my life.

BILLY, ALAN, *and* WALTER *come back into the room.*

ALAN: Ready to go, dear?

CHARLOTTE: Just let me put my accoutrement away.

ALAN: Can you believe I married a woman who carries a cigarette holder? Do you know how this goes over in Indiana?

LYSSA: I'm sure much better than me.

ALAN: No. There's the first female football coach at Notre
Dame. She prefers you to Chubby. But she's the only one.
He kisses her. See you tomorrow, Mousey.

BILLY: I'd suggest you wear feminine attire tomorrow. Maybe
a bow or headband in your hair. Talk about your mother.
How much you miss her. You've had a tough time but
you're a survivor. Women respond to that. And if he brings
up choice, do your father a favor and just soft-pedal it.
Wait till you get into office. Pleasure meeting you both.

WALTER: Mr. Robbins, don't worry. My wife is a rational
woman. This job is very important to her.

BILLY: See you tomorrow.

BILLY, ALAN, *and* CHARLOTTE *exit.*

LYSSA: Charlotte says this is putting a terrible strain on Dad.

WALTER: Lyssa, this is not about your father.

LYSSA: Oh, Walter, I'm a rational woman. I know what this is
and isn't about. God damn it, Walter! Would you stop
smoking? I don't want the housewives of Indiana hating
me for that too.

WALTER: Take it easy. You're making this all much harder than
it has to be.

LYSSA: I never meant for our life to become about me.
BOY'S VOICE *from offstage:* Mom! Mom! C'mere. Someone in
  Alaska hates you. You gotta c'mere!
WALTER: Lizard, please, let me try to help you.
BOY'S VOICE: Mom.
WALTER: I promise. We can get through this.
BOY: Mom, they think you're what's wrong with America.

LYSSA *and* WALTER *go upstairs.*

Sunday morning. Cameras, lights, and cable are being brought into LYSSA*'s living room.* TIMBER *acts as his own producer and is directing their placement. We can hear* QUINCY *on television.*

WOMAN: Quincy Quince, why has the "Lyssa Dent Hughes problem" sparked such a heated national debate?

QUINCY: Women are always reduced into categories, and in this case the "icebox cakes and cheese pimento canapé" moms are justifiably furious at having their life choices minimized. Now, I don't think for a minute that was Dr. Hughes's intention, but that's certainly where this story is going.

Equipment is still being moved. JUDITH *enters from upstairs.*

TIMBER: Thanks for letting me squeeze this in, Dr. Kaufman.

JUDITH: Lyssa Hughes is my oldest friend.

TIMBER: Chances are we'll do very well with her interview. Probably beat *60 Minutes*. There's a lot of interest in jury-gate.

JUDITH: If Dr. Hughes were a man, this wouldn't beat road

runner cartoons. It'd be a non-issue, an oversight. They'd
blame it on the maid or a wife.

TIMBER: You think wives are still willing to take the blame?

JUDITH: Have you ever been married, Timber?

TIMBER: No, ma'am. I have fear of intimacy and commitment.
Double negative and lethal.

JUDITH: Don't go into therapy, Timber. Stay just the way you
are.

TIMBER: Have you ever been married?

JUDITH: I've been married.

CREW PERSON: Where do you want her?

TIMBER: We're set up over here.

MORROW *enters.*

MORROW: Are they shooting Hollywood Squares here today?
I'll take center square.

JUDITH: Well, good morrow, Morrow.

MORROW: Do you know how many times I had to hear that
in high school? And of course To Morrow and To Morrow
and To Morrow.

JUDITH: You must have gone to a good high school!

MORROW: Timber, are you back by invitation?

TIMBER: I'm interviewing Lyssa this afternoon.

JUDITH: Morrow, are you back by invitation?

MORROW: Where's Walter? I've got good news.

JUDITH: Walter and Lyssa are upstairs getting ready for the
interview.

MORROW: How are they doing?

JUDITH: Why don't you go up and ask?

MORROW: I think we've got Harrison and Demi for the movie.

TIMBER: What movie?

MORROW: My movie.

JUDITH: Who's Harrison and Demi?

MORROW: Don't tell her if she doesn't know. God, I despise those Hollywood people. They're going to the White House for dinner tonight, so they had me give them ten-minute summaries of Jefferson and Tocqueville.

JUDITH: Do they think the President will give them a pop quiz?

MORROW: They don't like to talk about Hollywood in front of civilians. They prefer to talk about government or art. For instance, they all have opinions about Lyssa.

TIMBER: Like what?

MORROW: She's boring. She should only wear Armani. She has no sex appeal. She's the reason movies about smart women don't get made.

JUDITH: Can we please do this now? I have appointments.

TIMBER: Are we ready, Jimmy?

MORROW: What are we doing?

TIMBER: Dr. Kaufman has consented to go one-on-one with me. A sort of taped prelude to my interview with Lyssa.

JUDITH: Sit down, Morrow.

JIMMY: Ready?

TIMBER: Hold the work.

JIMMY: Quiet!

CREW PERSON: Quiet!

MORROW: What about hair and makeup? I insist on hair and makeup for Dr. Kaufman.

JUDITH: I already have hair and makeup.

TIMBER: Please, sit down, Morrow.

JIMMY: Ready?

MORROW *on the side:* Ready.

TIMBER *to camera person:* Just stay tight on Dr. Kaufman.

CAMERA PERSON: We're rolling.

TIMBER: I'm talking to Dr. Judith B. Kaufman, Professor of Oncology at Georgetown Medical School and a senior physician at its breast cancer unit. Thank you for joining us, Doctor.

JUDITH: My pleasure.

TIMBER: Dr. Kaufman, how long have you known the nominee?

JUDITH: We went to high school at Farmington. We met in a production of *Julius Caesar*. I was Calpurnia and she was Portia.

TIMBER: Interesting foreshadowing of political betrayal.

JUDITH: We also had a girl group at dances called "The Lyssettes." We sang "And then he kissed me." Lyssa had a great stage presence. I did not. I'm more of a behind-the-scenes person.

TIMBER: And how are you "behind the scenes" in Dr. Hughes's embattled nomination? You know that national opinion is running five to one against her.

JUDITH: Timber, when I was a girl in Brooklyn and I looked around for women I wanted to grow up to be, the only noteworthies I could muster were Mamie Eisenhower, and I knew chances were slim that I'd marry a President or grow bangs; Dorothy Killgallen, she wore a rhinestone eye mask on *What's My Line*—and I liked that; and Lena Horne, and I liked to sing, my mother was a pianist, but "And Then He Kissed Me" was as good as I got. I was a smart girl and I knew I wanted to grow up to be a scientist, but the only woman who even came close to my aspirations was Marie Curie. So I had to make up for myself who I was going to be.

TIMBER: Dr. Kaufman . . .

JUDITH: I believe by denying Lyssa Hughes this post we will be denying the country the talents of a remarkably concerned and inventive public servant, but also denying the girls of America someone they could, with pride, imagine themselves growing up to be.

TIMBER: What about failing to respond to the now infamous jury notice? Is that an action you would encourage in young women?

JUDITH: Who does your taxes, Mr. Tucker?

TIMBER: My accountant.

JUDITH: Who does your mail?

TIMBER: My secretary.

JUDITH: Who does your housecleaning?

TIMBER: Dr. Kaufman, who is the interviewer here?

JUDITH: Stay with me on this, Timber. Who does your house-keeping?

TIMBER: My housekeeper.

JUDITH: Any of them ever misplace a piece of paper?

TIMBER: Then why this outburst, this outcry against Lyssa Dent Hughes? Is this feminist backlash? Has she become, as Quincy Quince says, a "disempowered victim"?

JUDITH: I think we've got more serious issues here than trumped-up trends created by a would-be best-selling author.

TIMBER: Last question. As her best friend what advice would you give Dr. Hughes right now?

JUDITH:

"As you ramble on through life, brother,
Whatever be your goal,
Keep your eye upon the doughnut
And not upon the hole."

TIMBER: Advice that's good for all of us. Thank you, Dr. Judith B. Kaufman.

JUDITH: Thank you, Mr. Timber Tucker.

JIMMY: Let's set up for a reverse.

TIMBER: No. We don't need it.

SOUND MAN: I'm not sure we got that.

TIMBER: We'll be fine. Thanks, Dr. Kaufman. Very helpful. You obviously came well prepared. Jimmy ...

JIMMY: Where's Frank? We're going to have to knock back that sunlight.

TIMBER *and* JIMMY *exit.*

MORROW: Can I say something? Just one thing. The Mayflower Donut Shop, 59th Street and Fifth.

JUDITH: You weren't even born when they closed.

MORROW: I collect fifties retro. That motto is on my favorite set of mugs. I thought you were great. Really terrific.

JUDITH: Can I say something?

MORROW: Sure.

JUDITH: Why the hell did you do this to Walter and Lyssa?

MORROW: I was just making a point. Like writing a column. I forgot they were people I know and like.

JUDITH: That must be hard to live with.

MORROW: All right. I had eaten Twinkies ten minutes before. My blood sugar was up. The camera made me do it. What do you want me to say, Judith? I didn't know this would happen.

JUDITH: I don't feel sorry for you.

MORROW: Me either. I don't respect guilt. It's much too common. But I did endorse a healthy portion of my Harrison and Demi signing-on bonus as a donation to the Judith B. Kaufman oncology unit. It's not a new wing but it's still a very nice plaque. And the first time my largesse has not been for my own cause.

JUDITH: Morrow, I think you're bright enough to know it all goes smoother with a little redemption. Well, I certainly won't be used as your easy way out.

MORROW: Judith!

JUDITH: What?

MORROW: Would you have dinner with me sometime?

JUDITH: Morrow, if you've got a serious mother hang-up, I can refer you to a few numbers.

MORROW: I'm just looking for dinner or a conversation between Christians and Jews now and then.

JUDITH: Why?

MORROW: Because I was a smart boy. I had to make up for myself who I was going to be.

JUDITH: You didn't want to be Marie Curie either?

MORROW: No, but Dorothy Killgallen was a genuine possibility. Judith, think of the trips we could take together to avoid family gatherings and holidays.

JUDITH: Morrow, I have the career of a fifty-five-year-old man, the infertile reproductive cycle of a forty-two-year-old woman, and the emotional stability of a fifteen-year-old girl. I don't need any more stimulation. I hope you make that donation and I hope you get my name the fuck off of it.

TIMBER *reenters with* JIMMY.

JUDITH: Thank you, Timber. Good morrow, Morrow. *She exits.*

TIMBER: That's a very angry woman.

MORROW: That's a very good woman.

TIMBER: I heard you got Charlie Rose a three share Friday night.

MORROW: This all could have been avoided. You didn't have

to run that piece. Lyssa's an earnest public servant. And she'd be a fine Surgeon General.

TIMBER: I think so. That's why if I was them I wouldn't let you back in my house.

MORROW: Lyssa and Walter are my best friends.

TIMBER: Maybe I'm just a non-Ivy League TV news guy, but what I saw here last week didn't look like friendship to me. I'm curious—is there anything people like you really believe in?

MORROW: Let's see ... I have my faith, my seasonal venison sausage at London's Bibendum Restaurant, the films of Keanu Reeves, and my Glenn Gould recordings of the *Goldberg Variations*. Those are really the only things people "like me" believe in. And of course my three share on Charlie Rose. But people like you don't care about that at all. People like you are in it for the truth.

WALTER *enters from upstairs.*

MORROW: Hello, Walter. Good luck with the interview. *He exits.*

WALTER: What did he want?

TIMBER: I don't think he has any idea what he wants.

WALTER: Lyssa's almost ready.

TIMBER: We're not quite set up yet.

QUINCY *enters.*

TIMBER: You're early.

QUINCY: Am I?

TIMBER: Let's get going, Jimmy. *He exits.*

WALTER: Why are you here?

QUINCY: Didn't you know? I'll be commenting with Timber right after the taping.

WALTER: No, I didn't.

QUINCY: It's a real zoo in front of your house. Even Teddy Kenwright's here with a crew.

WALTER: The Nazi from the Renaissance Weekend?

QUINCY: He's doing the male perspective for Jim Lehrer's *News Hour.*

WALTER: Why can't Jim Lehrer do the male perspective?

QUINCY: Walter, you might not understand how important this has become. The buzz is that the President will have to go personally to the wall to save Lyssa or he'll be forced to pull her down. This is a very big deal.

WALTER: Apparently now so are you.

QUINCY: Well, actually, I was wondering if you could arrange for me to spend some time alone with Lyssa before the taping. I mean, she'd be much better off talking to me than to one of the TV hunks or beauty queens.

WALTER: Quincy, my wife won't talk to you.

QUINCY: Why not?

WALTER: Are you serious?

QUINCY: But I'm the one who can advance her cause.

WALTER: About as much as my former roommate Ted Kramer, the *New York Times* columnist, who called for the immediate withdrawal of Lyssa's nomination.

QUINCY: I don't think you appreciate what I'm doing for Lyssa. Whether she gets this job or not, she's still gotten a lot of heat out of it. And there'll be lectures, books; she can do science commentary.

WALTER: You're a lot tougher than she is.

QUINCY: I hope that's not a negative.

WALTER: My wife is not a "get," Quincy. I won't help you.

QUINCY: Hey, Walter, I hope this isn't about the other night, because ...

WALTER: You've got your commitments now and I've got mine.

LYSSA *enters. She is wearing a pastel suit, a little dowdy, and a headband.*

WALTER: You look great, Lizard.

QUINCY: You don't think the headband is a little much?

WALTER: It's perfect. Quincy's commenting after the interview.

LYSSA: Of course.

QUINCY: How are you holding up?

LYSSA: You seem to be the expert on me these days. How do you think I'm holding up?

WALTER: Honey, lets go outside and let them take some pictures.

WALTER *and* LYSSA *start towards the door.*

QUINCY: Lyssa, can I have some time alone with you now?

WALTER *to* QUINCY: What did I just tell you ...

LYSSA: No, Walter, I want to talk to Quincy.

WALTER: You don't have to do this.

LYSSA: I'm fine.

WALTER *exits to study.*

QUINCY: It looks like you and Walter have come to some decisions. Maybe it's none of my business ...

LYSSA: I am your business. I'm sorry.

QUINCY: Listen, I can think of a lot of reasons why you

wouldn't like me. But it's not good for any of us to watch an established icon being hung out to dry.

LYSSA: You know, the last time I wore a headband was at a Miss Porter's School dance in 1967. *She takes off the headband.* But I had a crush on Tommy Talbott from Hotchkiss and Tommy liked the girls who played lacrosse, wore "Ladybug" dresses and headbands. So the night he showed up at a Miss Porter's dance I put one on.

QUINCY: And did he like it?

LYSSA: Loved it. We went out for the next two years. And whenever I got back from a date I'd pull that headband right off my head. My best friends were not the lacrosse girls that Tommy Talbott preferred. My friends were much more sensitive. They lit incense and stayed up all night reading Rilke. But what was odd about me was that the headband girls thought I was one of them and the girls who wouldn't be caught dead wearing one would swear I was one of them too. Quincy, I'm a senator's daughter. So I can put it on and I can take it off. I haven't had to do it for a long time. I thought I had earned the right not to. But I won't be hung out to dry, Quincy, even if I have to wear a headband, bake cookies, or sing lullabies to do it.

TIMBER *and* WALTER *come in.*

TIMBER: We're almost set up, Quincy. *To* LYSSA. You're looking tidy, Dr. Hughes.

LYSSA: I'm feeling tidy.

QUINCY: Maybe a little too tidy.

TIMBER: This will all be fairly straightforward. I'll ask you a mix of questions about this past week. How you're dealing with the pressure. A little bit about your family. A little bit more about your politics.

LYSSA: Do we have to talk about my family?

TIMBER: Yes, but you can divert me. Here's a tip. If you get emotional, go for it. Don't hold back the tears.

LYSSA: Yes, sir. I'm doing double doses of estrogen in preparation. Ooooooooops. I'll be good. I promise. *She gets up.* Excuse me. I'm going to say hello to our friends on our doorstep.

LYSSA *and* WALTER *exit.*

QUINCY: You think she looks tidy? She bears no resemblance to who she is.

TIMBER: Relax. That's her business.

QUINCY: I need some advice, Timber.

TIMBER: Yes, ma'am.

QUINCY: Actually, I was hoping we could talk about it later. We probably both could use some time to unwind.

TIMBER: I never unwind.

QUINCY: *Time Zone* has expressed an interest in me for a permanent position.

TIMBER: Really? Women's issues? Personal profiles? It helps to get started by spending time in the field.

QUINCY: Actually, they offered me an exclusive on that fanatic at Legal Seafood.

TIMBER: Really? When did they do that?

QUINCY: Today. But what are, like, the chances for your show to survive? The buzz is, before Lyssa Hughes, *Time Zone* wasn't long for this world.

TIMBER: Don't go into television, Quincy. Stay pure.

QUINCY: No, I'm into it. I'm totally psyched.

As final preparations are taking place for the interview, we hear:

ANNOUNCER: *Time Zone* with Timber Tucker, Rachel Sullivan, Gabe Riehle, Madaline Smith, and special correspondent Quincy Quince. Tonight: a *Time Zone* exclusive, "An American Daughter," the Lyssa Dent Hughes interview continues. Part 2: "Jurygate."

Mid-Sunday afternoon. WALTER, LYSSA, *and* ALAN *are being interviewed by* TIMBER. CHARLOTTE, QUINCY, *and* BILLY *are present, along with television crew.*

CAMERA PERSON 1 *begins count:* And we're rolling. 1... 2...3...

CAMERA PERSONS 1 & 2: 4...5...

CAMERA PERSON 2: We have sync.

TIMBER: Tonight, a *Time Zone* exclusive, "An American Daughter," a family under siege. We are at the Georgetown home of Dr. Lyssa Dent Hughes, with her husband, Dr. Walter Abrahmson, Professor of Sociology at Georgetown

University, and her father, Senator Alan Hughes of Indiana.
Thank you for letting us into your home, Dr. Hughes.

LYSSA: My pleasure.

TIMBER: Walter, is your wife one of those remarkable young
women who does everything right?

WALTER: I'm a very fortunate man. My wife insists on spending as much time as possible with me and our twin boys.
I still don't know how she survives on five hours' sleep a
night. But she'll give up her own sleep before she'll ever
give up our family time.

TIMBER: Do you sleep more than your wife?

WALTER: My wife gets up at 5 A.M. to exercise. I'm crazy,
Timber, but I'm not that crazy. I like to run in the daylight.
But last summer Lyssa and our sons and I went wilderness
hiking in Montana. And I have to admit there was something incredibly inspiring about watching the sunrise with
all the family together.

TIMBER: Senator, how has this past week been for you? There
is mounting pressure from your colleagues in the Senate
and from women's groups, on both the left and the right,
for the President to withdraw her name from nomination.

ALAN: Timber, I've been a senator for twenty-four years and
a congressman for eight years before that. But first of all,
I am a father. Lyssa and I don't see eye to eye on most
issues, except coleslaw—we both like it dry—but there is
no one I believe in more.

TIMBER: But your daughter committed a crime.

ALAN: My daughter committed an oversight.

TIMBER: Senator, you and Lyssa are the fourth- and fifth-
generation descendants of Ulysses Grant. Grant was a man
whose public life was not always within legal limits.

ALAN: Grant was a great general. He was also a man. He made
bad investments, he drank, and some say he even screwed

up Reconstruction. There are people who believe the race situation in this country would be moved forward at least one hundred years if the Grant administration had moved quicker. But, of course, the race situation would be intolerable if General Grant hadn't moved at all. We're human, Timber; that's what's so timeless about Grant: his foibles are our foibles. He was a great American hero, imperfect just like all of us.

TIMBER: Is that how you think your daughter, Lyssa, at this moment should be looked at?

ALAN: I can't speak for my daughter. I haven't since she was five.

TIMBER: Walter, how has the past week changed your life?

WALTER: This week we've done a lot of talking and a lot of holding hands and just being there like old married couples do. I'm not ordinarily a religious man, but I have to admit I joined my wife last week in praying. If anything, actually, the events of the past week have brought us even closer. So for that, in some way, I'm grateful.

TIMBER: Do you think your wife's embattled nomination is indicative of the conflict inherent in liberalism and your "greening of America" generation?

WALTER: Let's not get academic here, Timber. Lyssa and I are just two real people who happen to be in a little trouble.

LYSSA: I made a mistake. I should have answered the notice. It was an oversight. And I apologize. It was simply bad juggling by a working mother.

TIMBER: Have you heard from the President, Dr. Hughes?

LYSSA: No. But this has been a very busy week for him. As you know, John Major is in Washington. We enjoyed your interview with him last night. And of course, as my father could tell you, the battle to balance the budget is ongoing.

ALAN: I believe the President knows he made the best possible choice when he nominated my daughter. The President is a man with good family values and, just like me, he knows what it means to be a father and be so deeply proud of your daughter. I look at this remarkable doctor and remember a little girl I drove to dancing class. We must honor all our talented American women.

TIMBER: So here you are, Lyssa Dent Hughes, descendant of a president, one of the leading professional women of your generation, a pioneer in health care reform, truly an American daughter of the highest caliber, in the midst of one of the great democratic and feminist maelstroms of this year. Who are the good guys and who are the bad guys?

LYSSA: I don't look at things in black and white. It's not even really good medicine. If there's any fault, it's mine. As I said, I made a mistake. I was wrong. I take full responsibility. Like my dad said, "We all have our foibles."

TIMBER: Female public opinion is running against you four to one. Why?

LYSSA: I don't know. I was honestly surprised by that. Most of my work in medicine has been in increasing awareness of women's health issues.

TIMBER: When you refer to women's health issues, are you referring to your position on choice?

LYSSA: Reproductive rights is one of many issues. For instance, primary care doctors are twice as likely to refer men to medical specialists while women of the same age and with identical symptoms and health histories are referred to psychotherapists. The ...

TIMBER: But you are pro-choice.

LYSSA: Yes.

TIMBER: And your father is not.

LYSSA: My father and I have differing opinions on many topics, except coleslaw.

"So here you are, Lyssa Dent Hughes, descendant of a president, one of the leading professional women of your generation, a pioneer in health care reform, truly an American daughter of the highest caliber, in the midst of one of the great democratic and feminist maelstroms of this year."

(Peter Reigert, Kate Nelligan, Hal Holbrook)

TIMBER: Do you consider yourself close to your father and his fourth wife?

LYSSA: Yes. I'm very happy my father met Chubby. I mean Charlotte.

TIMBER: Were you close to all of your father's wives?

LYSSA: I was away at college when he married Fay Francine. And I was a resident when he married Ginger Eichenberger.

TIMBER: So you weren't close to them?

LYSSA: They seemed to be nice women. But I was beginning my own life.

TIMBER: You have been for the past ten years on *The Ladies' Home Journal* list of American Women Role Models. Is that what makes women envious of you? Are you too perfect?

LYSSA: I hope not.

TIMBER: But you are privileged?

LYSSA: My greatest privilege is my family.

TIMBER: Let's talk some more about your family. Your mother?

LYSSA: My mother died when I was fourteen.

TIMBER: When we last talked, you referred to your mother as an ordinary Indiana housewife who made the now infamous "icebox" cakes.

LYSSA: Yes. My mother enjoyed baking.

TIMBER: Last time we spoke, you said she didn't bake the cakes. You said she put them in the icebox.

LYSSA: Yes.

TIMBER: What else can you tell us about her?

LYSSA: She was an attractive woman. She went to church.

TIMBER: Some might ask, did you resent her?

LYSSA: No.

TIMBER: Did you feel her horizons were limited?

LYSSA: How is this relevant to my confirmation?

TIMBER: Many women in America feel your attitude towards your mother is your attitude towards them.

LYSSA: I promise you. It's not.

TIMBER: Well, were you always closer to your father than your mother?

LYSSA: My father and I have both chosen to have careers in public life.

TIMBER: Did your father's career in public life cause your mother to suffer like so many political wives? Many famous political wives battled substance abuse.

LYSSA: Timber, I don't believe we can really judge who will make the best Surgeon General based on their mother's marital happiness.

TIMBER: But you and your husband agree that family life is important.

LYSSA: Yes, of course it's important. But it's also private.

TIMBER: The Surgeon General is considered the physician to the nation. Many American women feel that your private life disqualifies you for such an important humanitarian position.

LYSSA: How would they possibly know about my private life?

TIMBER: They are convinced, at least according to our latest *Time Zone* poll, that you are both condescending and elitist.

LYSSA: The women of America should concern themselves with the possibility of their reproductive rights being taken away from them. The women of America should concern themselves with the fact that breast cancer, ovarian cancer, and uterine cancer research is grossly underfunded compared with prostate cancer. The women of America should concern themselves that their children are increasingly smoking, falling prey to drug addiction and to the rapid growth of teenage pregnancy. The women of America should not concern themselves with my father's wives, my cooking, or my mother.

TIMBER: So you're emotional on this subject.

LYSSA: Yes, I share that with the women of America. I'm emotional.

WALTER: My wife is a very committed doctor.

LYSSA: Would you like to know, Timber, why I have avoided public life until this nomination? Because I know I can make a difference in the world without going through any of this. I know if I raise money for a walk-in clinic where there never has been one, it'll make a difference. I know I can take a splinter out of my son's hand and make a difference. The people I work with look at life and death every day. Sometimes we manage to save life and sometimes we don't. But it has nothing to do with whether we did or didn't like our mothers. It has to do with service.

TIMBER: Dr. Hughes, are you saying you're not fit for public life?

LYSSA: I'm saying I don't know what public life has become.

TIMBER: You mean you're too good for it?

LYSSA: There's nothing quite so satisfying as erasing the professional competency of a woman, is there? Especially when there's such an attractive personal little hook to hang it on. Oh, we all understand it now! She must have hated her mother! That's why she's such a good doctor. She must be a bad cold person. That's why she achieved so much. And anyway it would be all right if she were a man and cold. That man would be tough. No one would give a damn what he felt about his mother! But a woman? A woman from good schools and a good family? That kind of woman should be perfect! And if she manages to be perfect, then there is something distorted and condescending about her.

"There's nothing quote so satisfying as erasing the professional competency of a woman, is there?" (Kate Nelligan)

That kind of hard-working woman deserves to be hung out to dry. That's a parable the Indiana housewives can tell their daughters with pride. They can say for those of you girls who thought the Lyssa Dent Hughes generation made any impact, you're wrong. Statistically they may have made an impact, but they're still twisting in the wind just like the rest of us.

TIMBER: How do you think the President will feel about this?

LYSSA: I really wouldn't know. I went to college with the President's wife. She's an intelligent, sensible person. She even has a sense of humor. But I can't speak about her opinion right now since neither she nor her husband has been in touch with me. But I'd be happy to take their call.

TIMBER: How do you think they will react to tonight's interview?

LYSSA: How do you think they'll react, Timber?

TIMBER: Senator, would you call your daughter's challenge to the President "unconditional surrender"?

LYSSA *takes off her headband and microphone.*

LYSSA: I think I've completed this interview.

TIMBER: Tonight, Lyssa Dent Hughes defends her nomination to the women of America. From all of us here at *Time Zone,* thanks for joining us.

Lights go off and the crew strikes cameras, lights, and cables. There is a long pause before anyone speaks.

TIMBER: I'm sorry it turned out this way. I tried to warn you.

LYSSA: I appreciate it.

QUINCY: You got it. You really heard me, didn't you? That was fantastic. Is there anything else you want to add before I comment on it outside?

LYSSA: No. I've said what I have to say.

QUINCY: Good-bye, Mrs. Hughes, Senator.

She exits.

ALAN: I think I might like to mention this to a few colleagues before they watch it tonight. Is that all right with you, Lyssa?

LYSSA: Sure.

ALAN: Just as a courtesy to our young friend Billy Robbins?

LYSSA: Are you all right, Dad?

ALAN: I'm fine, if you are.

LYSSA: Bye, Dad. Bye, Chubby.

CHARLOTTE: Good-bye, dear. I'm so proud of my husband.

She and the SENATOR *exit.*

TIMBER: I don't suppose you'd like to do a follow-up?

LYSSA: I don't think so, Timber.

TIMBER: Have I ever told you my chaos theory of broadcasting?

LYSSA: No.

TIMBER: Whatever is happening this moment won't be happening three minutes later. So, in the long run, how important is it?

LYSSA: To the person it happened to, it's a lifetime. It's a whole memoir.

TIMBER: We're just going to do a wrap-up outside, and then we'll be out of your hair.

He exits, followed by the crew and the last of the television equipment.

WALTER: And that's the ball game.

LYSSA: Are you angry?

WALTER: No. I'm just waiting to hear from the President. Maybe we should go to a movie.

LYSSA: I'm tired, Walter.

WALTER: The boys were looking forward to seeing you on television. They'll be really disappointed. How will we explain this to them?

LYSSA: Oh, I'll just say life's unfair. The good guy doesn't always win. Being good at school doesn't necessarily mean you're so good at life. Something encouraging like that.

WALTER: I'm sorry I couldn't help you.

LYSSA: You tried.

WALTER: I thought you were great. Really magnificent. Your finest hour.

LYSSA: Judith says I don't know what it is to want. Well, I really wanted that job, Walter. I would have been good.

WALTER: We're smart people, Lizard. We deserve to have gotten everything out of it that the really smart ones get.

LYSSA: I don't know what "really smart" means anymore. Maybe Quincy's really smart. Did you sleep with her?

WALTER: Why did you wait till now to ask me?

LYSSA: I was busy. Jury duty.

WALTER: I'm sorry.

LYSSA: Me too. I'm sorry we couldn't have broken this to Timber. The women of America might have become quite sympathetic.

WALTER: I feel like I'm disappearing, Lizard. I don't know who I'm supposed to want to be anymore.

LYSSA: Walter, this was my nomination. Can we please not make it your humiliation?

She exits.

Late Sunday afternoon, dusk. WALTER *is listening to the Beach Boys singing "Wouldn't It Be Nice." He opens the blinds and light pours in the windows.* JUDITH *enters from the garden.*

JUDITH: I told you not to leave the gate open. Any kind of manic-depressive meshuganah could just waltz in here.

WALTER: Do you like the Beach Boys, Judith? I find them unbelievably moving. Maybe it's because I grew up in Woodmere, Long Island, so they bring back nothing from my childhood.

JUDITH: I prefer the early song cycles of Marvin Gaye and Tammy Tyrrell. I just heard on an instant radio poll that the women of America, four to one, want the President to have a dog instead of a cat. *She turns off the music.* Walter, you study the patterns of American life. Can you explain something to me?

WALTER: I don't know if I'm the one to explain this. Good vibrations, yes. The women of America, no.

JUDITH: Just tell me how come there still seems to be a club and once you're admitted there are practically no rules or limitations. But to gain admission, certain applicants have to meet requirements that would make the most honorable member fall flat on his face.

WALTER: I've been working here on another question, Judith. Do you think the man who nominated your best friend, a good, well-educated man who reminds us so much of ourselves, is in fact far more insidious than someone who hates every goddamn thing we believe in?

While he is speaking, LYSSA *walks into the room.*

LYSSA: Why don't you ask your panel tonight, Walter? I'm sure they'll have plenty of opinions.

JUDITH: Is tonight "Wanted Dead or Alive"?

WALTER: I was planning to skip it. Stay home with my wife.

LYSSA: Don't skip it, Walter. I could be the subject of the final debate, instead of my father's position on choice. At least we'll keep it in the family. Walter, you're going to be late if you don't get changed.

WALTER: Judith, I hope you know how much we both appreciate your friendship. *He exits upstairs.*

JUDITH: He's in a generous mood.

LYSSA: Is the Festival of Regrets still going on? I've got a coffee cake I might want to toss into the Potomac. I surrendered, Judy. At 4:26 Eastern Standard Time, I called the President and withdrew.

JUDITH: I know. I heard it on the radio, as I was driving back from my last farewell to 1147. Just about the same time you called the President, my final quest for fertility collapsed.

LYSSA: Oh, God. I'm sorry.

JUDITH: Aren't you even a little impressed with our timing? I was. So, I began to count my blessings. My years of sitting in doctors' offices surrounded by snapshots of children I'll never bear were over, and so was your hideous ordeal.

LYSSA: So now what do we do?

JUDITH: Personally, if I can't make life or stop death I've got some time on my hands for friendship. This will pass, honey, I promise.

LYSSA: And badda-bing-badda-boom I turn into a sandwich.

JUDITH: What?

LYSSA: Just another useless allegory I learned along the way.

ALAN *comes in, dressed in black tie.*

ALAN: The reporters' vans have all pulled away. We won't have to serve refreshments. And I was hoping to do a swift business in souvenirs.

JUDITH: See, I'm right. No one will remember.

ALAN: Yes, they will. They'll remember it was bad. But they just won't be sure why.

JUDITH: I have to go. I'm on call. Lookin' good, Senator.

ALAN: Are you off to more services? They're certainly keeping you busy.

JUDITH: No. I'm on call at the hospital. I've already had the answers to my prayers. I prefer the reliable variables of science. I'm going back to work. *She kisses* LYSSA. Good night, honey. Take care of her, Senator. *She exits.*

ALAN: I thought I'd have supper with you and the boys tonight.

LYSSA: In black tie? No wonder Walter says I'm too attached to you!

ALAN: Actually, I thought I'd offer, you'd decline, and I'd escort Chubby to a fund-raiser for the Lab School, glad a few hands, allow Chubby to display her accoutrement, and, overall, put on a fairly good front. Mousey, why didn't you call me before you withdrew?

LYSSA: I don't know. Would Ulysses have called his father? I made a quick assessment. The Commander-in-Chief thanked me for moving so quickly.

ALAN: You know that I would have stood by you no matter what.

LYSSA: You tried, Dad. You're off the hook. I'm the one who didn't heed the ancient wisdom of Billy Robbins.

ALAN: I figured out why. You read too many of those girl books about Eleanor Roosevelt and Florence Nightingale when you were young. I should have found you heroines who were more sensible, people like Arianna Huffington and Amy Fisher.

LYSSA: You withheld privy information. You never told me it was going to be this hard.

ALAN: You never asked.

LYSSA: Did I tell you I got a telegram from a leather-goods company asking me to do an ad on horseback? "Ulysses S. Grant's fifth-generation granddaughter charges into battle with a Doone & Burkey purse."

ALAN: Was it a nice purse?

LYSSA: It was a handbag. A little olive green and horsey for my taste. But perhaps Chubby would like it.

ALAN: Perhaps. She's turned out to be a rather good sport. Fourth time around I think I've managed to find a partner who actually protects me.

LYSSA: Maybe you should train her to bite. Sorry, Dad.

ALAN: You weren't like this in high school. I remember you as very sweet.

LYSSA: You sent me away to high school.

ALAN: After this term, Chubby and I have decided to take off for six months to visit her born-again golf-pro son in Sydney while I begin my memoirs. And if no one's interested in the memoirs of an old coot, I was thinking we could open an enchanting little pharmacy in Fort Wayne. I'd whip up the home remedies and Chubby would peddle her darling Eva's face cream. Maybe I could even sing a little country and western on the weekends.

LYSSA: And did you come to this conclusion in the past week?

ALAN: Jesus, I can't put anything over on you.

LYSSA: No. My daddy taught me to pay attention.

ALAN: Before Ulysses Grant became President, he gave a speech before Congress confessing that he wasn't particularly prepared for the Presidency. But he was perfectly happy to stay in the White House for two terms because he wasn't particularly prepared for anything else either. Do you think I should stick around just because there's nothing else this old man can particularly do?

LYSSA: What about your principles?

ALAN: My principles! There's some idea of America out there right now that I just can't grab onto. I know I'm supposed to have opinions based on the latest polls, and not personal convictions or civil debate. It doesn't intimidate me. But it's certainly not our most illuminating or honest hour. With time getting short, I'd rather shoot the cattle than run for Congress.

LYSSA: Dad, do you remember when I was in elementary school, every two years just in time for your next election, you'd buy me a red Chesterfield coat? It was the only time you and I ever went shopping together.

ALAN: That was a classy coat.

LYSSA: It was classy for a five-year-old, and I was going on twelve. That coat was a red badge of wool. Every other kid in the school had a normal pea jacket or green parka. I even hid it in a shopping bag at school and said I was holding it for my cousin Maimie.

ALAN: But you took it out from storage for campaigns.

LYSSA: Always. Lyssa in red. Shaking hands, passing brochures.

ALAN: Until you began telling the electorate you didn't support your candidate.

LYSSA: I developed a conscience about both the content and the garment. But you know what's so stupid?

ALAN: You're anything but stupid.

LYSSA: No, I promise this is stupid. I was sitting here before, thinking I'd give anything for you to show up and say, "Everything's going to be fine. Here's an awful red coat."

ALAN: Mousey ...

LYSSA: Did I ever tell you I hated that name even more than the red coat? I don't know. Other people ...

ALAN: Other people what, Mousey?

LYSSA: Other people might just know better.

ALAN: You mean other people might know better than to put themselves in a situation where everything might not be fine. I looked at you this afternoon, and I wished your mother could have known even for one night what it's like to be as strong and courageous as you.

LYSSA: Dad, did you love her?

ALAN: Your mother was a very bright and complicated person. If she were an ordinary Indiana housewife, she might have been in a lot less pain. I loved her very much.... Oh, wait. I didn't come empty-handed. An auctioneer from Chicago called me when you were first nominated. He said he had something that might interest you. It's a letter from Ulysses to his daughter, Ellen Wrenshell Grant. It's dated Cold Harbor, Virginia, June 4, 1864. Shall I read it?

LYSSA: Please.

ALAN: "My dear little Nelly, I received your pretty well-written letter today in my camp. You do not know how happy it made feel to see how well my little girl not yet nine years old could write."

LYSSA: Dad.

ALAN: Gets better. "Your mother wrote that you no longer wish to portray the Old Woman That Lived in a Shoe at the fair. Dear Nelly, there are times when I don't wish to go on either. We've been fighting now for thirty days and have every prospect of more fighting to do before we get into Richmond. It seems to me, for both of us, our task is to rise and continue. Look after your mother, study your lessons and you will be contented and happy. Love, Papa." *He gives her the letter.* Bye, Mousey. *He walks to the door.*

LYSSA: Dad, Nelly Grant's life was a disaster. Her parents married her off to a philandering British adventurer. She was divorced, with four children, by thirty-five.

ALAN: Our family is American and has been for generations. *He exits.*

BOY'S VOICE: Mom. Mom. There's a person in Portland who says that you're honorable and there's a person in Pittsburgh who says that you're not. What should we do?

WALTER *enters.*

WALTER *to* KIDS: I'll tell her. *To* LYSSA: The kids want you to answer questions upstairs. They say you've got a chat room exploding in Pittsburgh.

LYSSA: Yes. It sounds like Pittsburgh's a rebel stronghold.

WALTER: Lizard, I can still skip my panel. Stay home and answer them.

LYSSA: No, I'll get there. You better get going, or liberalism will live or die without you.

WALTER: I'm afraid you won't be here when I get back.

LYSSA: Where would I go tonight?

"It seems to me, for both of us, our task is to rise and continue."
(Hal Holbrook)

WALTER: I don't know. It makes no sense. I'm just afraid, like one of our kids.

LYSSA: Don't be afraid, Walter. I'll be here when you get home.

WALTER *exits through the garden.* LYSSA *looks at the letter.*

BOY'S VOICE: Mom, Pittsburgh wants to talk to you now! What should we tell them? Mom!

LYSSA: "Our task is to rise and continue." *She stands and glances out the window as she walks upstairs.* Prepare, gentlemen, for toppling Pittsburgh like a house of cards!